A GUIDE
to the
BOOKSTORES
of
TORONTO

A GUIDE
to the
BOOKSTORES
of
TORONTO

Arthur B. Wenk

P. Warren-Wenk

ECW PRESS

CANADIAN CATALOGUING IN PUBLICATION DATA

Warren-Wenk, P. (Peggy)
A guide to the bookstores of Toronto

Includes index.
ISBN 1-55022-288-0

1. Bookstores – Ontario – Toronto Metropolitan Area – Directories.
1. Wenk, Arthur B., 1943–   .   II. Title.

Z488.6.T67W3 1996   381′.45002′025713541   C96-931181-8

Imaging by ECW Type & Art, Oakville, Ontario.
Printed and bound by Webcom, Scarborough, Ontario.

Distributed in Canada by General Distribution Services,
30 Lesmill Road, Don Mills, Ontario M3B 2T6.
Order desk: (800) 387-0141 (Ontario and Quebec),
(800) 387-0172 (other provinces), FAX (416) 445-5967

Published by ECW PRESS,
2120 Queen Street East, Suite 200,
Toronto, Ontario M4E 1E2.

For Adriana,
*who made sure we visited
playgrounds as well as bookstores*

To write a book is easy. It requires only pen and ink and the ever-patient paper. To print books is a little more difficult because genius so often rejoices in illegible handwriting. To read books is more difficult still, because of the tendency to go to sleep. But the most difficult task of all that a mortal man can embark on is to sell a book.

— Sign in Steven Temple Books from a poem by
Felix Dahn, paraphrased by Sir Stanley Unwin

Never lend books — nobody ever returns them; the only books I have in my library are those which people have lent me.

— Anatole France

If a book is worth reading, it is worth buying.

— John Ruskin

Table of Contents

Preface

The purpose of this book is to acquaint book lovers with the remarkable array of bookstores in the city of Toronto (with a sampling of interesting bookstores in the surrounding region). There are some 250 bookstores in the city, not counting individual members of chains. They include general, specialty, used, rare, and mail-order stores, with a good deal of overlapping among these categories, and range in size from tiny neighbourhood comic-book stores to megastores.

In addition to fine general and secondhand bookshops, the city offers stores specializing in automobiles, bridge, cookbooks, dance, film, music, mysteries, numismatics, pets, sailing, science, and woodworking. There are foreign language stores carrying books in Chinese, Ethiopian, French, Hungarian, Italian, Korean, Latvian, Portuguese, Russian, Serbian, Spanish, Ukrainian, and Vietnamese, as well as a bookstore specializing in English-as-a-second-language. A bookstore reflects the unique character of its neighbourhood: Harbord Street or Queen Street West or Mirvish Village, Mt. Pleasant Avenue, Little Italy, Chinatown, the Beaches or Old Cabbagetown. We hope you will experience the ambience of Third World Books & Crafts Inc. or Negev Book and Gift Store, savour the aura of The Occult Shop or The Omega Centre, appreciate the displays at Charles Mus Gallery or New Ballenford Books or Art Metropole, admire the mascots at The Lion, the Witch and the Wardrobe or Hairy Tarantula Comics and Cards Ltd., or simply relax and browse at Writers and Company or Nicholas Hoare. Even the smallest neighbourhood bookstore mirrors the taste of the people and the community it serves.

A bookstore, for the purposes of this project, denotes an establishment primarily in the business of selling books. Thus, we have not included variety stores, convenience stores, stationery stores, or book sections of department stores. We have included major university bookstores but not the book centre for every educational institution. We have included the principal denominational bookstores but not the bookroom of every individual church. We have also included those museum stores where the book collection offered a unique subject specialty.

There is a distinction between fine antiquarian books and used books. However, we have decided not to draw this distinction in the subject organization of this directory because antiquarian and used books are normally sold in the same establishment.

In an effort to make this guide as complete as possible, we have consulted articles on bookstores in various Canadian magazines and journals, *The Book Trade in Canada*, 1994; *Sheppard's Book Dealers in North America: A Directory of Secondhand and Antiquarian Book*

Dealers in the U.S.A. and Canada, 1993; the *Toronto & Area Directory of Antiquarian Booksellers*; and the Toronto Yellow Pages.

For each bookstore, a telephone interview elicited the information contained in the first half of the entry, while a visit led to the descriptive paragraph in the latter half. (For the bookstores listed as Mail-Order, we requested sample catalogues and carried on more extended interviews by telephone.) We then mailed a copy of the text to each bookstore to request corrections or additions. We would welcome additional comments from those who use this book.

In addition to cooperation from the city's booksellers, we gratefully acknowledge the assistance of Christopher Wan and Tommy Kong, who guided us through Toronto's Chinese-language bookstores, and Clifford McCarthy, who shared his expertise on comic-book stores with us.

The first epigraph at the beginning of this book has a dark side. Rising real estate prices in Toronto and a prolonged recession have contributed to the demise of more than seventy bookstores during the course of this project. We include a list of establishments that have closed or moved out of the city. *Requiescat in pace.*

September 1996

Guide to Use

This book consists of three sections:

- Lists of the bookstores included in this directory: retail stores in Toronto; mail-order stores in the Toronto area; and selected out-of-town bookstores within a day's drive of Toronto. Also included is a list of those stores that have recently ceased retail operation.

- The main body, with a description of each bookstore, divided into three categories: retail stores, mail-order stores, and out-of-town stores.

- Indexes, including a geographical index and an index by subject specialty.

Each entry gives the name and address of the bookstore, the nearest cross-street, telephone number, fax number and e-mail address where applicable, specialty, owner's name, approximate size (small: under 10,000 volumes; medium: 10,000–50,000 volumes; large: more than 50,000 volumes), special services provided, special events occurring at the bookstore, directions on getting there by public transportation, a note on parking, and a 100–200 word description of the bookstore. (To make the prose flow more easily, we have adopted an authorial "I" in writing these narrative descriptions.)

The bookstores are arranged alphabetically within each section according to the following rules: entries are arranged word-by-word, not letter-by-letter (e.g., *Book Mark* comes before *Bookman*); acronyms or names beginning with letters appear first (e.g., *DRB Motors* comes before *David Mason Books*); numbers come at the beginning (e.g., *1,000,000 Comix* comes before *ABC Bookstore*); bookstores named for persons are listed by the full name of the store (e.g., *Albert Britnell Book Shop*, with a cross-reference included under *Britnell*); the character "&" is treated as "and."

Introduction

Definition of Terms

"Books," as denoted in this guide, include volumes new and used, hardcover and paperback, comic books, antiquarian books, and books on tape. A few words may be in order to acquaint the reader with other terms used in this guide:

- ANTIQUARIAN BOOKS depend for their value on the quality of their paper, binding, illustrations, first editions signed by the author, and their relative rarity.

- AUDIOBOOKS, or books recorded on audio cassettes, generally present abridged versions of the original text, read either by the author or by a professional actor or actress.

- COMIC BOOKS have flourished in their current format since World War II. Collectors divide early comics into Golden Age (from around 1945 to 1956) and Silver Age (from 1956, the start of the superhero series, to around 1970). The price for new issues should not vary from store to store. For back issues, the *Overstreet Price Guide* provides one of the most accurate sources of information. (In order to provide a basis of comparison among stores, we checked which titles were available beginning with the letter "S.")

- GAMING refers to role-playing games, beginning with "Dungeons and Dragons," which, over the last two decades, have spawned a subgenre of instructional books.

- GRAPHIC NOVELS consist of extended narratives, portrayed in comic-book style and presented in large-format, hardbound or trade paperback books.

- MASS-MARKET PAPERBACKS refer to inexpensively produced, softbound editions.

- REMAINDER BOOKS, or publisher's overstock, are new books offered at substantial discounts in order to clear an inventory.

- TRADE PAPERBACKS, as compared to mass market, are printed in larger format on superior quality paper and with better bindings.

Bookstores and the Internet

As we go to press, bookstores are acquiring e-mail addresses with the same rapidity that they previously acquired fax numbers. We have included as many e-mail addresses as possible, but more stores will have them by the time you read these words. A few stores have also established a presence on the World Wide Web, and we have included their Uniform Resource Locators (URLS). Uniquely digital bookstores have already begun to appear. Toronto has two, which we have placed in the Mail-Order section of this guide.

- Brief remarks on a number of Toronto bookstores may be found on the Internet at http://www.math.uio.no/faq/books/stores/north-american/northern.html

- A guide to locating the names of bookstores, without descriptions, may be found at http://www.toronto.com/surfin/stores/books.html

Personal Favourites

Here are a few bookstores we particularly enjoy:

- CHILDREN'S BOOKSTORES: Children's Book Store; The Constant Reader; Mabel's Fables

- OTHER SPECIALTY BOOKSTORES: Anglican Book Centre; Atticus Books; Caversham Book-sellers; Champlain Book Store; The Cookbook Store; Hollywood Canteen; Parentbooks; Science City Science Book Stores; The Sleuth of Baker Street; Theatrebooks; Toronto Women's Book Store

- GENERAL BOOKSTORES: Albert Britnell Book Shop; Bob Miller Book Room; Book City; The Book Company; A Different Drummer; Nicholas Hoare Bookstore; This Ain't The Rosedale Library; University of Toronto Bookstore; World's Biggest Bookstore; Writers and Company

- USED AND ANTIQUARIAN BOOKSTORES: Abelard Books; Annex Books; Batta Book Store; David Mason Books; Eliot's Bookshop; Half Price Books and Music; Ten Editions Book-store; Village Book Store

Local Book Festivals and Sales

- Canadian Children's Book Week (early November; Canadian Children's Book Centre, 35 Spadina Road, Toronto, Ontario M5R 2S9, telephone 416-975-0010, fax 416-975-1839)

- International Festival of Authors (mid-October of each year; Harbourfront Reading Series, 410 Queens Quay West, Suite 100, Toronto, Ontario M5V 2Z4, telephone 416-973-4760)

- Toronto Antiquarian Bookfair (Wesley Begg, Contact Editions, telephone 416-322-0777, fax 416-322-3225)

- University of Toronto Book Sale (April and October of each year; run by the University of Toronto Graduate School Union, telephone 416-978-2391)

- Word on the Street (last Sunday of each September; contact Caroline Taylor, telephone 416-504-7241)

Serial Publications on the Canadian Book Trade

The following publications are available at most libraries:

- *The Book Trade in Canada with Who's Where; L'industrie du livre au Canada avec Où trouver qui*. Manotick, Ontario: Ampersand Communications. A directory of publishers and booksellers in Canada. Useful information on the Canadian book industry in general. Published annually.

- *Books in Canada*. Toronto: Canadian Review of Books. "A national review of books" which began in 1971. Scholarly articles. Published 9 times/year.

- *The Canadian Bookseller*. Toronto: The Canadian Booksellers Association. This magazine on booksellers and bookselling in Canada begain in 1888, and is "devoted to the interest of the book, stationery and fancy goods trade." Published 10 times/year.

- *Canadian Books in Print*. Toronto: University of Toronto Press. Indexes by author, title, subject, and publisher. Lists current Canadian publications, primarily of works in English, but also includes French-language publications by English-language publishers. Published annually, with updates.

- *The Literary Review of Canada*. Toronto: Literary Review of Canada. A scholarly journal publishing essays on "Canadian books on culture, politics and society." Contributors are well-known Canadian academics and authors. Begun in 1991. Published 11 times/year. Similar in format to the *Times Literary Supplement* or the *New York Review of Books*.

- *Les livres disponibles canadiens de langue française: Canadian French Books in Print*. Outre-mont, Québec: Bibliodata. A directory of current French-language books in print in Quebec and Canada. In addition to its author, title, and subject indexes, includes a list of French-language publishers in Canada. Published annually.

- *Quill & Quire*. Toronto: Key Publishers. "Canada's magazine of book news and reviews." Begun in 1935, this magazine publishes reviews of Canadian books, especially literature, and provides short articles on the Canadian book trade. Published monthly.

LISTS OF BOOKSTORES

The Bookstores

This section includes lists of retail, mail-order, and out-of-town bookstores, followed by a list of stores that have recently ceased retail operation.

Retail Bookstores in Toronto

Mail-Order Bookstores

Out-of-Town Bookstores

Ceased Retail Operation

Abbey Bookshop
All Continents Company
Alladin's
Ann's Bookstore and Mostly Mysteries
Aurispa Books
Ben Abraham Books for the New Age
Blackie's Books
Book Bargains, Inc.
Bookfinder, The
Book Factory, Inc.
Book Sale, The
Book Sale Warehouse Outlet Store, The
Books and More
Books Books
Books on Bloor
Bookquest
Bookshuttle
Bookwork
Book Palace
Broadview Books
Bryan's Books
Buttercup Bookshop
Canadian Book Distributors
Canadian Books Express
Canadian Small Business Institute
Catholic Truth Society Book Centre
Century Home
The Comic Shoppe
Comic Zone
Common Knowledge Books, Etc.
Cover to Cover Books
Central Book Store
Diamond Starr Collectibles
Discount Cards and Comics
Dollars & Sense
Dundas Book Store

Electric Bookstore
German Book Store
Gotham Books and Comics
Hall of Heroes
Healthy Choices
Heritage Books
In Good Taste
Inadvance Products
International Bible Suppliers
J.G. Books
Joy Forever, A
Joy of Learning
Kanda Kawa Bookcentre
Leake Stones Used Book Store
Lexicon Polish Book Store
The Library Shoppe — Zoren Library Services, Inc.
Lindsay's Books for Children
Longhouse Bookshop, Ltd.
Maiden Mother Crone
Martin Books, J.A.
Marxist-Leninist Party of Canada
Niagara Rainbow Crafts, Inc.
Page Turners
Phoenix Comics
Progress Books
Queen's Comics and Memorabilia
Rainbow Books for Children
Sun Sun Book Store
Superheroes Comic Books
That Other Bookstore
Topper Books
Tung Ying
Unknown Worlds
Ukrainski Knyha Divison of Demo Trade Ltd.
World Bookstore Co.

RETAIL BOOKSTORES
IN TORONTO

100th MONKEY OASIS

66 Wellesley Street East
(2nd floor; between Yonge and Church)
Toronto, Ontario M4Y 1G2
416-925-7633 (FAX 416-495-1604)

SPECIALTY: Esoteric, therapeutic and creative
("E.T.C.") ideas/events
OWNER: Alexander Chua and the "E.T.C."
Cooperative
SIZE: Small (2,500 titles, books, videos, and
audiotapes)
SPECIAL SERVICES: Bibliotherapy, mail orders,
special orders
SPECIAL EVENTS: "E.T.C." circles, lectures, and
readings
GETTING THERE: Wellesley subway station;
parking behind building

The 100th Monkey, named after Ken Keyes's book of
that title, creates a meditative space with its large
Chinese wall hanging, occult prints above the bookshelves, and New Age music in the background. The
store divides its offerings into three main categories —
esoteric, therapeutic, and creative — with books
on astrology, dreams, dying and grief, Gurdjieff-
Ouspensky, hermetic-alchemical, holistic living,
Kabbalah, occult fiction, paranormal, self-expression,
subtle body, transpersonal and cognitive psychologies,
and yoga. There are additional sections on non-western
religions (Hindu, Buddhist, Tibetan, Taoist, Theo-
sophical, Sufi, Islam). The store also sells environmental music tapes.

1,000,000 COMIX

513B Yonge Street
(near Wellesley)
Toronto, Ontario M4Y 1Y3
416-944-3016 (No FAX)

SPECIALTY: Comic books, sports cards, toys, posters
OWNER: Andy, Chris, and Kostos Giancoulas
SIZE: Large
SPECIAL SERVICES: Memberships offering regular
customers 20% discounts on back issues
SPECIAL EVENTS: Sales
GETTING THERE: College or Wellesley subway
station on Yonge line; municipal parking lot on
Wellesley

Toronto has some two dozen bookstores devoted to the
sale of comic books, serving a clientele composed primarily of males aged sixteen to thirty. Their stock
encompasses current mainstream comics, alternative or
small-press comics, and collectors items from the Golden
(1945–1956) and Silver Age (1956–1970). More than two
hundred different comics are published each month in
North America by half a dozen mainline publishers.
Popular heros such as Spiderman or Superman may
have four different comics published each month with
related titles. Because of the prolific nature of the genre,
comic-book stores have to be extremely selective in the
titles they will carry on a regular basis. 1,000,000
Comix specializes in comic books of the Silver Age and
displays a signed and numbered copy of *Dark Knight*,
selling for $350, a Marvel Comics edition of *Strange
Tales* which originally sold for 12¢, now worth $150,
and an early copy of *Amazing Spiderman* for $250. The
store carries a great number of current comics, mostly
mainline, as well as graphic novels, posters, cards, and
miniatures.

ABC BOOKSTORE

662 Yonge Street
(near Charles)
Toronto, Ontario M4Y 2A4
416-967-7654 (No fax)

SPECIALTY: Used books and magazines
OWNER: Loch McKay
SIZE: Medium (around 30,000 titles)
SPECIAL SERVICES: N/A
SPECIAL EVENTS: N/A
GETTING THERE: Just south of Yonge/Bloor subway station; municipal parking lot one block away

ABC Bookstore exemplifies the "omnium gatherum" philosophy of the neighbourhood used bookstore that provides a home for every stray book. Fiction, mostly mass-market paperbacks, occupies a large section in the middle of the store and covers the usual categories, from adventure to westerns. The store also offers non-fiction hardbacks in a variety of subjects, as well as a large collection of old and vintage magazines for its Yonge Street clientele, with *Life* and *Vogue* at the front, and *Hustler*, *Playboy*, *Penthouse*, *Gallery*, etc., kept discreetly in back.

ABELARD BOOKS

519 Queen Street West
(near Spadina)
Toronto, Ontario M5V 2B4
416-504-2665 (No fax)

SPECIALTY: Serious non-fiction, theology, philosophy, medieval studies, literature, art, archaeology, and rare books in these subjects
OWNER: Paul Lockwood
SIZE: Large
SPECIAL SERVICES: N/A
SPECIAL EVENTS: N/A
GETTING THERE: Queen Street steetcar; municipal parking lot ½ block away

Queen Street West boasts Toronto's largest concentration of used and rare bookstores. Along this venerable corridor, David Mason, Jamie Fraser, McBurnie and Cutler, Robert Wright, and Steven Temple have all established highly respected bookstores. Abelard Books presents a serious collection of mostly hardbound books, chosen with discriminating taste, displayed in bookcases ten shelves high, and classified with wooden labels into categories ranging from anthropology and architecture to theology and travel. On a recent visit, antiquarian books in glass-covered display cases included John Locke, *The Reasonableness of Christianity*, London, 1695, *The Works of Francis Bacon*, published in 1778, and *Chaucer's Works*, published in London in 1721. Comfortable sofas and reading chairs encourage customers to peruse their selections at leisure.

ABOUT BOOKS

83 Harbord Street (near Spadina)
Toronto, Ontario M5S 1G4
416-975-2668 (FAX same)
e-mail: aboutbks@inforamp.net

SPECIALTY: Scholarly, antiquarian, and general secondhand, hardcover, and paperback
OWNER: Mrs. A. Greenwood
SIZE: Medium
SPECIAL SERVICES: Appraisals
SPECIAL EVENTS: N/A
GETTING THERE: Spadina subway station; parking on street

Sidewalk stalls containing bargain books (50¢ to $5) and a black cat at the door welcome visitors to About Books, a large, well-organized store selling used books, both hardbound and paperback. Its principal areas of concentration lie in history (one entire room, filled floor to ceiling), literature, and sciences. Other categories include architecture, automobiles, cooking, film, foreign language (with a large section of books in French), gardening, industrial history, linguistics, marine, military, music, mythology, philosophy, poetry, railroads, religion, social sciences, and social history. They also have antiquarian books in many subjects. The store purchases large and small collections of hardcover and paperback books from individuals and from estates.

ACADIA BOOK STORE

232 Queen Street East
(near Sherbourne and Queen)
Toronto, Ontario M5A 1S3
416-364-7638 (FAX 416-364-1446)

SPECIALTY: Art and illustrated books, general scholarly and rare books
OWNER: Asher Joram
SIZE: Medium (30,000 to 40,000 titles)
SPECIAL SERVICES: N/A
SPECIAL EVENTS: N/A
GETTING THERE: Queen Street streetcar; parking on street

Acadia Art and Rare Books has a large stock now devoted exclusively to out-of-print and secondhand art books. The store carries many monographs on a wide range of artists, as well as books on architecture, artists' biographies, Canadian art, exhibition catalogues, graphic design, photography, sculpture, technique books, and rare and limited edition art books with original lithographs. The upper floors of Acadia are devoted to rare books, leather bindings, older books, as well as a large stock of antique prints, which include botanical, architectural, historical maps, fashion prints, etc. The owners are always interested in purchasing art books (single books and collections).

ACTIVE MINDS

Chapters Inc. Head Office
90 Ronson Drive
Rexdale, Ontario M9W 1C1
416-243-3138 (FAX 416-243-8964)

SPECIALTY: Children's educational books and toys
OWNER: Chapters Inc.
SIZE: Small
SPECIAL SERVICES: Special orders
SPECIAL EVENTS: Theme-related activities; for Space Month, for example, there was a Model Magic Workshop, Lego Playday, and Make a Comet Book Mark

Active Minds describes itself as "a treasure house of books for infants to 12 year olds, where learning is child's play." Each branch contains toys, educational materials, and a considerable number of books, classified into active readers, babies and toddlers, hobbies, I Can Read, people and places, pop-up books, reference, rhymes and poems, and workbooks. There is a large collection of storybooks, arranged facing out and overlapping on the shelves, books on tape and video, and all the major series for youngsters: Hardy Boys, Nancy Drew, Apple Fiction, Sweet Valley Kids, and many other sets. The store contains a section of books in French, as well as a multicultural section.

Store locations in the Metro Toronto area include Fairview Mall (1800 Sheppard Avenue East, Willowdale, 416-498-1307), and Erin Mills Town Centre (5100 Erin Mills Parkway, Mississauga, 905-569-3607).

THE AEROMART INC.

3679 Dundas Street West
(near Jane)
Toronto, Ontario M6S 2T3
416-769-9429 (FAX 416-269-9492)

SPECIALTY: Aviation
OWNER: Lois Apperley, Manager
SIZE: Small
SPECIAL SERVICES: Special orders
SPECIAL EVENTS: Displays at aviation and aircraft shows
GETTING THERE: Jane subway station on Bloor line, bus to Dundas; parking in driveway

The Aeromart provides aviation supplies, including flight suits, gauges, polyester reinforcing type, aircraft finishes, pilots' logbooks, and videos. A member of the Canadian Booksellers Association, it offers a small, very specialized collection of books on aviation such as *Avionic Systems, Automatic Flight Control, How to Become an FAA Air Traffic Controller, Aircraft Gas Turbine Powerplants Workbook, The Beginner's Guide to Flight Instruction*, and *Low-Horsepower Fun Aircraft You Can Build*. One can also find illustrated books on particular aircraft.

ALBERT BRITNELL BOOK SHOP

765 Yonge Street (at Bloor)
Toronto, Ontario M4W 2G6
416-924-3321 or 1-800-387-1417
(FAX 416-924-3383)
e-mail: jab@io.org
http://www.io.org/~jab/jordan.htm

SPECIALTY: Excellent general trade bookstore, strengths in recent non-fiction, biography, children's books
OWNER: Mary Britnell-Fisher; Betsy Britnell, general manager
SIZE: Medium (40,000 titles)
SPECIAL SERVICES: Special orders, discount cards, out-of-print searches, mail orders to anywhere in the world
SPECIAL EVENTS: Signings
GETTING THERE: Bloor/Yonge subway station; parking at municipal lot on Cumberland

Britnell's is a wonderful bookstore to visit, not only because it has so many fine books one would like to read, but also because you will likely happen upon books you hadn't known about, books that seize your attention and make an impassioned plea to be read. Happily, Britnell's encourages browsing, and on the shelves of its dark wood bookcases, elegantly labelled with black lettering on brass, one will find a large but careful selection of books in biography, business, children's books, fine arts, history, recent fiction and non-fiction, reference, and travel, with smaller numbers of books in many other categories. There are also several tables of remaindered books.

In business for over 100 years, Britnell's is Toronto's oldest bookstore, but it features all the most recent technology, including ordering by fax or e-mail, and a web site.

ALEPH BET JUDAICA INC.

3453 Bathurst Avenue
(between Lawrence and Wilson)
Toronto, Ontario M6A 2C5
416-781-2133 (FAX 416-781-1311)

SPECIALTY: Judaica
OWNER: Moshe Joseph
SIZE: Medium
SPECIAL SERVICES: Mail orders
SPECIAL EVENTS: N/A
GETTING THERE: Bus from Bathurst station on Bloor subway line; parking in front of store

Aleph Bet Judaica carries a wide variety of books in both Hebrew and English. A shelf of commentaries in English includes Chumash commentary, Chumashim, Midrashim, Talmud studies, Tanach commentary, and Torah anthology. Multivolume sets of commentaries and holy books in Hebrew occupy a wall at the rear of the store. In addition, Aleph Bet Judaica offers an extensive collection of books for children and young adults, dictionaries, pedagogical tools, devotional books, and books on history, as well as cassettes, gifts, and Hebrew-language newspapers.

ALEXANDRE FINE ANTIQUE MAPS AND BOOKS

104 Queen Street East (near Jarvis)
Toronto, Ontario M5C 1S6
416-364-2376 (FAX 416-364-8909)

SPECIALTY: Antiquarian plate books
OWNER: Alexandre Shahram Arjomand
SIZE: Small (500 books)
SPECIAL SERVICES: Book searches
SPECIAL EVENTS: N/A
GETTING THERE: Queen Street streetcar; parking on street

Located in a neighbourhood dominated by electronics stores and pawn shops, Alexandre Fine Antique Maps and Books occupies a large, well-lighted room displaying antique prints and maps. The book collection, displayed on six low shelves, is tiny but very precious. One's attention is drawn to a volume of Hogarth's works standing almost three feet high, next to books on travel and topography, architecture, militaria, rare prints and maps, and illustrated books from the 17th to 19th centuries with an average price of between $500 and $5,000.

ALFSEN HOUSE BOOKS

154 Main Street North
(Markham Road and Route 7)
Markham, Ontario L3P 1Y3
905-294-2571 (No FAX)

SPECIALTY: General secondhand store
OWNER: Andrew Alfsen and Adam Alfsen
SIZE: Medium (30,000 books)
SPECIAL SERVICES: N/A
SPECIAL EVENTS: Occasional sales
GETTING THERE: Markham bus or GO bus; parking behind store and on street

Alfsen House Books is a general used bookstore selling formerly popular books in well-used paperback editions or better-preserved hardcover editions. The bulk of the collection consists of mass-market paperbacks geared to light reading — animals, biographies, children's books, classics, comics, general fiction, history, mysteries, science fiction, and self-help, with some collectibles and remainders.

ALTERED STATES COMICS

1900 Lakeshore Road (Inverness Plaza)
Mississauga, Ontario L5J 1J4
905-855-1288 (No FAX)

SPECIALTY: Comics
OWNER: Doug Kerr and Dave Kerr
SIZE: Medium to large (around 75,000 comics)
SPECIAL SERVICES: Buy and sell, evaluate condition of used comics
SPECIAL EVENTS: Once a month, different artists sign their work
GETTING THERE: Mississauga Transit; parking in front of store

The vast majority of current comic books in North America come from three or four publishers, but there are also alternative comics with much smaller press runs. Altered States Comics, in addition to carrying current issues of the usual popular comics, sells the publications of a number of small, independent comic-book companies not found in most comic-book stores. Under "S" I noted *Saga of the Submariner, Solo Avenger, Sabretooth, Saga of Crystal Warrior, Secret Witch, Semper Fi, Sleeze Brothers, Speedball, Starriors, Street-Poet-Ray, Strike Force Morituri*, and *Swords of the Swashbuckler*, most of which I had not seen elsewhere. The store also carries gaming books, a number of videos, and used comic books going back to the early 1960s.

ALTERNATE GRAVITY

230 Queen Street (near John)
Toronto, Ontario M5V 1Z6
416-598-4237 (FAX 416-588-5464)

SPECIALTY: Comics
OWNER: Logan Lubera
SIZE: Small
SPECIAL SERVICES: Reserve, searches
SPECIAL EVENTS: Games days, autograph signings
GETTING THERE: Queen Street streetcar; parking on street

Many comic-book stores carry miniatures and gaming materials as a sideline, but no store in Toronto goes further in this regard than Alternate Gravity. The store regularly invites people from the industry to hold painting seminars, draw comics, and sign books. The second-floor rental studios offer a working and learning environment for local artists, one of whom was giving a model-painting demonstration when I visited the store. Several gaming tables provide an arena for weekly tournaments. In addition to mainline comics, the store carries some Japanese comics in translation, graphic novels, and science fiction.

ANGLICAN BOOK CENTRE

600 Jarvis Street (south of Bloor)
Toronto, Ontario M4Y 2J6
416-924-9192, 416-924-1332, or
1-800-268-1168 (for out-of-town customers)
(FAX 416-924-2760)

SPECIALTY: Religious books, hymnals, church
furnishings, publications under the Anglican Book
Centre imprint
OWNER: Anglican Church
SIZE: Medium (25,000 titles)
SPECIAL SERVICES: Book searches, special orders
SPECIAL EVENTS: Author signings
GETTING THERE: Subway to Sherbourne or
Bloor/Yonge stations; free parking south of
building

The Anglican Book Centre is a well-stocked general
religious bookstore offering serious scholarly books as
well as popular treatments of theological topics. Both
professional theologians and interested laypeople will
find books on every aspect of the Christian faith: altar
guild and servers, Anglican Book Centre publications,
Anglicanism, Apocrypha, art, Bibles, Bible background, Bible study, biography, C.S. Lewis, children's
literature, children's prayers, Christian education,
Christian faith and life, commentaries, comparative
religion, cookbooks, death and dying, dictionaries,
drama, ethics, gift books, Greek-Hebrew, grief and
bereavement, healing, history, initiation, Judaism, lifestyles, literature, liturgy, ministry, music, native peoples,
New Testament, Old Testament, Orthodoxy, prayer
collections, prayer and spiritual life, prayerbooks, psychology, Roman Catholicism, sermons, social issues,
theology, women, and youth ministry. A room is
devoted to Christian education resources. The store
also carries church diaries, aids to prayer, calendars,
crosses, icons, religious artwork, giftware, classical CDs
and cassettes, and videos.

ANNABLE NURSERY LIMITED

5201 Highway 7
(near McCowan Road)
Unionville, Ontario L3R 1N3
905-477-1231 (FAX 905-477-1353)

SPECIALTY: Horticultural books for beginners to
professionals
OWNER: Bob Annable
SIZE: Small (700 titles)
SPECIAL SERVICES: Mail orders
SPECIAL EVENTS: N/A
GETTING THERE: Markahm Transit TTC; parking
on premises

The book room forms an adjunct to the principal
business, a nursery offering a full selection of trees,
plants, pots, and garden accessories. The small collection contains books on gardens, landscaping, pests,
pruning, shrubs, and trees, including such titles as *The
Organic Gardener's Handbook of Natural Insect and
Disease Control*, *Four Seasons of Bonsai*, *The World of
Northern Evergreens*, *Ferns to Know and Grow*, *The
Complete Book of Cacti and Succulents*, and *Thyme on
My Hands*. Beside the book room, in the main building,
you will find an unusually fine assortment of planting
pots in all sizes.

ANNEX BOOKS

1083 Bathurst Street
(near Dupont)
Toronto, Ontario M5R 3G8
416-537-1852 (No FAX)

SPECIALTY: General used and rare books, specializing in Canadian and modern literature and poetry; signed first editions
OWNER: Janet Fetherling
SIZE: Medium (25,000 titles)
SPECIAL SERVICES: Catalogues issued
SPECIAL EVENTS: N/A
GETTING THERE: Bathurst subway station, then bus north to Dupont; parking on street

Many of the used books at Annex Books seem practically new, since the owner receives a steady supply of review copies and books from regular customers who enjoy buying books but who live in small apartments. Light-coloured wooden bookcases running to the ceiling contain books on African studies, antiques, art, drama, English history, film, history, literature, media, music, mystery, philosophy, poetry, psychology, reference, science, the 60s, and women's studies. Literature, the largest category, includes special sections on Canadian literature, Canadian poetry, Vita Sackville-West, the English 20th-century writer, and David Gascoyne, the last of the surrealists. A number of interdisciplinary studies have been drawn together into a section entitled contemporary theory.

ANOTHER MAN'S POISON

29 McCaul Street (west of University between Queen and Dundas)
Toronto, Ontario M5T 1V7
416-593-6451 (FAX same)

SPECIALTY: Books on design: graphics, architecture, 20th-century design, antiques, collectibles, nostalgia
OWNER: Hollis G. Landauer
SIZE: Medium (10,000 titles)
SPECIAL SERVICES: Large worldwide stock, special orders, and search service
SPECIAL EVENTS: N/A
GETTING THERE: Subway to University and Queen; parking on street

Another Man's Poison is a comprehensive design bookstore, featuring historical and contemporary decorative and applied art, graphics, and architecture. Here you will find books on 50s Italian glass or Lalique, Chippendale or Arts & Crafts furniture, Derby or deco ceramics, poodle skirts and jewellery, toys, slot machines, radios and televisions, watches and pens, advertising and typography, T-shirts and CDs, residential and commercial architecture, diners and theatres. Another Man's Poison merits a visit even if you're not looking for a book, since the store is filled with period pieces: a jukebox, televisions, kitchen appliances, and toys. It would be difficult to fault the owner's claim to having the best design store in North America.

ANOTHER STORY

164 Danforth Avenue
(near Broadview)
Toronto, Ontario M4K 1N1
416-462-1104 (FAX 416-462-9115)

SPECIALTY: Children's books, anti-racist literature, feminist collections, social activism, labour, and native issues
OWNER: Sheila Koffman and Peter Legacy
SIZE: Small
SPECIAL SERVICES: Special orders; book tables at conferences; discounts to teachers; multicultural; anti-racist material for school boards
SPECIAL EVENTS: Book launches, poetry readings
GETTING THERE: Broadview subway station on Bloor line; parking lot near Broadview

As the name of the store suggests, Another Story is devoted to presenting alternative views on contemporary social issues. Many of the books displayed here will not be found in other bookstores in Toronto. In the music/poetry section, one encounters *The History of the Blues*; in literature, *The Heinemann Book of African Women's Poetry*; in ecology, *The Eros of Everyday Life: Essays on Ecology, Gender and Society*; in theology, *Reading Ruth: Country Women Reclaim a Sacred Story* and *Facing the World with Soul*; in labour, *Whose Brave New World? The Information Highway and the New Economy*. There are mysteries by women writers, children's books emphasizing Third World cultures and non-sexist contexts, books on gay and lesbian issues, and more than a hundred magazines not often sold in Canadian bookstores, including *Fireweed: A Feminist Quarterly*; *Seasons: The Environment and Water Magazines*; and *Alternate Press Review*.

ANSON-CARTWRIGHT BOOKS

229 College Street (near St. George)
Toronto, Ontario M5S 1R4
416-979-2441 (FAX same)

SPECIALTY: Rare books, Canadiana, modern literature, fine leather bindings, juveniles, maps and prints
OWNER: Hugh Anson-Cartwright
SIZE: Medium (10,000 titles, including storage)
SPECIAL SERVICES: Catalogues issued once or twice a year, customer want lists
SPECIAL EVENTS: N/A
GETTING THERE: Queen's Park subway station, College streetcar line; metered parking on street

Thirty years at this location, Hugh Anson-Cartwright has built a clientele of regular customers worldwide. An eclectic collector, he buys anything that interests him. He particularly likes books in fine bindings, rare voyages and travels, and books with special illustrations, such as those by Picasso and Matisse for the Limited Editions Club. In addition to selling books, Anson-Cartwright is one of the leading appraisers of books and archives donated to universities and museums.

ARKA UKRAINIAN BOOKS

575 Queen Street West
(between Spadina and Bathurst)
Toronto, Ontario M5V 2B6
416-366-7061 (FAX 416-366-0990)

SPECIALTY: Eastern European books and Ukrainian gifts
OWNER: Arka Ltd.
SIZE: Small (8,000 books)
SPECIAL SERVICES: Mail orders, special orders
SPECIAL EVENTS: N/A
GETTING THERE: Queen Street streetcar; parking on street

Arka Ukrainian Books offers a wide range of books in Ukrainian as well as English translations of Ukrainian authors. There are cookbooks in both languages, books on crafts, particularly Ukrainian Easter eggs, bilingual children's books, books on conversational Ukrainian and Ukrainian grammar, Ukrainian/English and Polish/English dictionaries, schoolbooks, music books, religious books, and tourist guides. The more recent books tend to be nationalistic in orientation, such as *Subjugated Natives: Their Struggle for Natural Liberation*, *The USSR Unmasked*, *The Black Deeds of the Kremlin*, and *Discordant Voices: The Non-Russian Soviet Literature*. There are a number of books dealing with the Ukrainian community in Canada, as well as Ukrainian newspapers, gifts, dolls, records, and CDs.

ART AND MIND

55 Bloor Street West
(at Bay and Bloor, in the concourse
level of the Manulife Centre)
Toronto, Ontario M4W 1A4
416-968-1511 (FAX 416-968-1087)

SPECIALTY: Books and gifts, architecture, design, fine art, photography, drawing, watercolour, origami, animation
OWNER: Dominic Riverso
SIZE: Small
SPECIAL SERVICES: N/A
SPECIAL EVENTS: N/A
GETTING THERE: Bay station on Bloor line or Yonge and Bloor station; two hours free parking in Manulife Parking garage

Art and Mind is designed to stimulate one's visual imagination. During a recent visit there were two dozen books on origami and eight on the art of M.C. Escher, along with books of optical illusions, op art, and games based on illusions. One finds books on aesthetics, architecture, books on particular artists, cartoons, colour, decorative arts, design, graphics, how-to-draw books for children, painting and drawing, photography (how-to books and volumes devoted to Man Ray, Robert Mapplethorpe, et al.), sketching, and sculpture, as well as lots of games, toys and amazements, guides to face-painting, costumes and hair-braiding, and art supplies for children. Rarely have I seen so many interesting books in such a small space.

ART GALLERY OF ONTARIO BOOK SHOP

317 Dundas Street West (at McCaul)
Toronto, Ontario M5T 1G4
416-979-6610 (FAX 416-979-6674)

SPECIALTY: Books on the visual arts, particularly fine arts, architecture, sculpture, design, and photography
OWNER: Art Gallery of Ontario
SIZE: Medium
SPECIAL SERVICES: Special orders, book searches
SPECIAL EVENTS: Special section reflective of current exhibitions in the AGO
GETTING THERE: St. Patrick subway station or Dundas Street streetcar; parking in Village-by-the-Grange

The Art Gallery of Ontario Book Shop, part of a very sizeable gallery store, occupies a spaciously attractive setting with comfortable sofas, high ceilings and wall-to-wall carpeting. The collection covers virtually every aspect of the visual arts: anatomy, architecture, art criticism (three bookcases), art history (four bookcases), artists (twelve bookcases), book arts, calligraphy, Canadian art (three bookcases), cartooning, cartoons and humour, colour theory, crafts, drawing, film, film criticism, gallery publications, museology, oil painting, painting technique and handbooks, pastel/acrylic, perspective, photography (four bookcases), printmaking, sculpture, teaching art, travel guides, and watercolour. The shop also offers a children's section, more than one hundred periodicals on the arts, as well as video cassettes on particular artists, CD-ROM titles with an art subject matter, and adult and children's audio compact discs.

ART METROPOLE

788 King Street West, 2nd Floor
(near Bathurst)
Toronto, Ontario M5V 1N6
416-703-4400 (FAX 416-703-4404)

SPECIALTY: Artists' bookworks, multiples, audio and video works
OWNER: Non-profit, artist-run centre
SIZE: Small (500 books)
SPECIAL SERVICES: Special orders
SPECIAL EVENTS: Exhibition openings, lectures
GETTING THERE: King Street streetcar; parking on street

Art Metropole specializes in contemporary Canadian and international art in non-traditional multiple media formats, with particular emphasis on post-1960 conceptually based work. The store sells artists' bookworks (books generated by artists), artists' multiples (small limited issue art objects), and artists' audio and visual works. Art Metropole's catalogue describes Robert The's *book gun* as "Artist's bookwork in the form of a handgun, cut with a jigsaw from a hardcover book, discarding the original text and book format to produce a book-gun." Under the heading of artists' multiples, the catalogue lists *Iron-On Labels*, by Dick Higgins, "a continuous strip of 10 iron-on labels, printed with the phrase, 'this is not an art work by me', and signed by the artist. Also included is a card with text. Packaged in a plastic envelope." The store exhibits other multiples such as T-shirts, buttons, inflatable tags and the like. The books often serve as a record of visual arts in various formats, including maps, sketches, etchings, photographs, poems, postcards, or combinations of formats. Art Metropole maintains an archive of conceptually based works, some of which are on display. This is a most remarkable, thought-provoking store well worth a visit.

ATTICUS BOOKS

84 Harbord Street
(near Spadina)
Toronto, Ontario M5S 1G5
416-922-6045 (FAX 416-926-9686)

SPECIALTY: Used scholarly books in all academic disciplines
MANAGER: Donald Smith
SIZE: Medium (35,000 titles)
SPECIAL SERVICES: N/A
SPECIAL EVENTS: N/A
GETTING THERE: Spadina subway station; metered parking on street

Of all the bookstores on the remarkable Harbord Street row, Atticus Books surely ranks as one of the most unusual. Any scholar can find something in his or her field of study, be it art history, Asian studies, classics, history and philosophy of science, history, linguistics, literature and criticism, mathematics, medieval and Renaissance studies, music, philosophy, psychology and psychoanalysis, or religion. At Atticus Books, you'll see everything from books on reindeer herding to a treatise on the French parody noël. Technically these are used books and are offered at 50–60% of list price, but one would scarcely know it by the appearance, for all the books look nearly new.

AUREUS INVESTMENTS

1240 Bay Street
(inside the 1240 Bay Shopping Mall)
Toronto, Ontario M5R 2A7
416-966-9108 (No FAX)

SPECIALTY: New and used books on ancient history, archaeology, and numismatics
OWNER: Gordon C. Kumpikevicius
SIZE: Small
SPECIAL SERVICES: Searches for out-of-print and used books
SPECIAL EVENTS: Periodic exhibitions of coins
GETTING THERE: Bay subway station on Bloor line; parking lots in area

Serious coin collectors, as distinguished from hobbyists, tend to know a good deal of history. In the case of classical numismatics — the collection of Greek, Roman, and Byzantine coins and medallions — the field of knowledge extends to archaeology as well as classical history. Those interested in coins from antiquity depend not only on books but also on sale catalogues to locate and price particular coins. Aureus Investments offers the largest Canadian inventory in this specialized domain. One will find books for beginners, such as *Illustrated Teach Yourself Coin Collecting*, but the collection focuses on studies such as *Historical Results from Bactrian Coins and Other Discoveries in Afghanistan* and *The Ancient Boeotians and the Coinage of Boeotia* as well as sale catalogues such as *Catalogue of the Important Collection of Anglo-Saxon Silver Pennies Formed by F. Elmore Jones*. Chief numismatist Gordon Kumpikevicius and book manager Mark Tooth issue catalogues several times a year.

AUTOPHILE

1685 Bayview Avenue
(near Eglinton)
Toronto, Ontario M4G 3C1
416-483-8898 (FAX same)

SPECIALTY: Books on automobiles and motorcycles
OWNER: Richard Stafferton
SIZE: Small
SPECIAL SERVICES: Mail orders, book searches
SPECIAL EVENTS: N/A
GETTING THERE: Eglinton subway station,
   Eglinton bus; parking on street

Autophile serves both those interested in cars for their own sake and those interested in what cars can do. For the latter group there are books on racing events, biographies of racers, and books on how to drive a car to get the most out of it. For the former group there are books such as *How to Rebuild Your Big Block Chevy*, *Ford Pick-ups 1932–1952*, *Camaro Restoration Handbook*, as well as parts books and coffee-table photograph books. The store also carries more than fifty current automobile magazines, collectors' miniature cars in several different formats, and car kits.

AVIATION WORLD

195 Carlingview Drive, Unit 11
(off Dixon Road)
Rexdale, Ontario M9W 5E8
416-674-5959 or 1-800-668-1987
(FAX 416-674-5915)

SPECIALTY: Books and magazines on airliners,
   civilian and military aircraft
OWNER: Len Neath
SIZE: Small
SPECIAL SERVICES: Mail orders, government
   aviation publications, tables at hobby shows
SPECIAL EVENTS: N/A
GETTING THERE: #58 bus from Lawrence West
   subway station, get off at Carlingview, and walk ½
   km. south; parking on premises

Aviation World stocks pilots' manuals, air traffic controller guides, airworthiness manuals, aircraft repair manuals, instructors' guides, pilot test preparation manuals, pilot's log books and world aircraft recognition handbooks, as well as histories of air power, airplane manufacturers, air shows, and air racing. There are illustrated books on individual aircraft, such as *Soviet Military Helicopters*, *Hercules: The C130 in Service*, and *F–4 Phantom: Guardian of the Free World*, and more than fifty magazines including *Jane's Defence Weekly*, *Plane and Pilot*, *Air Photographers International*, and *L'Aéroport*. Besides books, you will find pilot supplies, hobby supplies, travel accessories, aviation prints, aircraft display models, patches and stickers, posters, air band radios, and a variety of clothing and jewellery. Aviation World is the only bookstore in Toronto marked by a windsock.

B. BROUGHTON CO. LTD.

2105 Danforth Avenue
(near Woodbine)
Toronto, Ontario M4C 1K1
416-690-4777 or 1-800-268-4449
(FAX 416-690-5357)

SPECIALTY: Religious books, gift ideas, clergy apparel, and church supplies
OWNER: Brian Broughton
SIZE: Medium
SPECIAL SERVICES: Special orders
SPECIAL EVENTS: N/A
GETTING THERE: Woodbine subway station on the Bloor line; parking behind the store

B. Broughton Co. Ltd. offers a complete range of Roman Catholic literature in a spacious, comfortable setting with easy chairs provided for browsers. Categories include Bible study, Bibles, cassette talks, catechetics, children's liturgies, clip art for bulletin boards and banners, drama, education, family life, general (e.g., *Modern Saints: Their Lives and Faces*), homilies, ministries, music, pastoral resources, prayer, RCIA (Rite of Christian Initiatives of Adults), sacraments, scripture, social justice, and youth ministry. A substantial children's section displays books such as *More Little Visits with Jesus* and *Lifetimes: The Beautiful Way to Explain Death to Children*. The store also carries figurines, clerical apparel, and a complete supply of all church needs.

BJ'S PAPERBACK EXCHANGE

1236 Lawrence Avenue East
(two lights west of Victoria Park)
Toronto, Ontario M3A 1B9
416-447-3360 (No FAX)

SPECIALTY: Buys and sells paperback books on all subjects
OWNER: Gloria Ronahan
SIZE: Medium (15,000 to 20,000 titles)
SPECIAL SERVICES: N/A
SPECIAL EVENTS: N/A
GETTING THERE: Bus from Lawrence subway station; free parking in plaza

As the name suggests, BJ's Paperback Exchange specializes in light reading at bargain prices, with most of the books in very good condition. The store allows 15% on exchange, and resells books at 50% of their cover price, with mass-market paperback books arranged into adventure, biography and non-fiction, historical romance, humour, mystery, novels (including lots of Harlequin and Silhouette books), psychology and spirituality, science fiction, sports, and war. A second branch is located at Newtonbrook Plaza (5833 Yonge Street, 416-222-1955).

BAILEY'S CHRISTIAN SUPPLIES

3064 Dundas Street West
(near Keele)
Toronto, Ontario M6P 1Z7
416-767-7796 (FAX 416-767-7796)

SPECIALTY: Bibles, books, tapes, soundtracks, videos, gifts, cards
OWNER: Privately owned
SIZE: Small
SPECIAL SERVICES: N/A
SPECIAL EVENTS: N/A
GETTING THERE: Dundas subway station, then bus; parking on street

Bailey's Christian Supplies is a small store with an emphasis on evangelism. It sells Bibles in various translations, including a large-print version, the Basic Bible Commentary series, God's Word for Today series, Young Readers Christian Library series, and a small number of books on church history, Christian education, counselling, prophecy, and creation science. There are religious T-shirts, cassettes devoted both to worship and to country & western music, CDs featuring the Brooklyn Tabernacle Choir, music videos such as "Children's Heroes of the Bible: The Story of Elijah," and computer software to produce Bible verses on command.

BAKKA SCIENCE FICTION BOOK SHOPPE

282 Queen Street West (near Spadina)
Toronto, Ontario M5V 2A1
416-596-8161 (FAX 416-596-1218)
e-mail: jdrose@bakka.com

SPECIALTY: Used and new science fiction, fantasy, and horror
OWNER: John Rose
SIZE: Medium (10,000 titles)
SPECIAL SERVICES: N/A
SPECIAL EVENTS: Autographing, readings, and anniversary sale
GETTING THERE: Queen Street streetcar to Soho Street; metered parking on side streets

The name Bakka will be known to readers of Frank Herbert's *Dune* as the legendary weeper who mourns for all mankind. This is a store that takes care of its customers. A sign by the door reads, "Smokers will be eaten." The bookcases contain occasional notes to guide the browser (e.g., on *The Magic and the Healing*, "Yes, there are unicorns in it, but *The Magic and the Healing* is *not* a fluffy book. The veterinary medicine practiced in here is down and dirty — and also accurate. The emotional struggles of the main character aren't fluffy, either. Add on top of all that an easy writing style that pulls you right in, and you've got a definite winner"). The store carries new and used hardbound and paperback titles in science fiction, fantasy, and horror, with a large Star Trek section and a fair number of magazines. In business since 1972, Bakka is one of the oldest specialty stores in Canada, and one of the oldest science fiction stores in the world.

BALFOUR BOOKS

601 College Street
(near Clinton, west of Bathurst)
Toronto, Ontario M6G 1B5
416-531-9911 (FAX 416-531-5019)

SPECIALTY: General used and scholarly books and video rental
OWNER: Joyce Blair
SIZE: Medium
SPECIAL SERVICES: video rental: foreign films, classic films, independent films
SPECIAL EVENTS: N/A
GETTING THERE: College Street streetcar; parking on street

In the Little Italy section of Toronto, near Capitol Trattoria Pizzeria, Café Diplomatico, Caffé Bar Azzurri (but right across from the Golden Princess Theatre, featuring movies in Chinese), lies Balfour Books, a recent addition to the city's used book stores. The front windows feature changing displays: at the time of my visit, I saw cookbooks and books on spices, wines, desserts, etc., on one side, and a variety of offbeat books on the other, including independent and small press publications. Inside one finds bookcase-lined walls offering mostly hardcover books with their original dustjackets in the usual categories, ranging from archaeology to travel and women's studies. The store rents videos as well as selling books, in competition with a video store across the street featuring films in English, Italian, and Portuguese.

THE BATNER BOOKSTORE

180 Steeles West
(near Yonge Street)
Thornhill, Ontario L4J 2L1
905-731-4440 (FAX same)

SPECIALTY: textbooks (grades 1 to OAC), literature for book clubs, children's books, Judaica, general
OWNER: Corina Batner
SIZE: Medium
SPECIAL SERVICES: Textbooks for private schools, books for literary clubs
SPECIAL EVENTS: N/A
GETTING THERE: Finch subway station, Steeles West bus; parking in plaza

The Batner Bookstore has strengths in several areas. As a service to a local high school, it began to stock textbooks. The project snowballed and now brings in teachers from throughout the area for texts from grades 1 to OAC. The store also serves area literary clubs, some twenty-five to thirty years old, supplying multiple copies of books chosen by university professors or by members of the clubs. As a consequence, and reflecting the owner's own background, the store has a very strong literature section. The establishment also serves as a good neighbourhood bookstore, with offerings in art, biography, business, Canadian literature, Canadiana, children, cookbooks, fantasy and science fiction, health and fitness, inspirational books, Judaica, juvenile (four bookcases), mystery, New Age, parenting, poetry, popular science, psychology, reference, sports, war and history, women, and young adult. Readers on a budget will be particularly interested in the large number of trade paperbacks in fiction.

BATTA BOOK STORE

710 The Queensway
(near Royal York Road)
Toronto, Ontario M8Y 1L3
416-259-2618 (No FAX)

SPECIALTY: General used books with an emphasis
on literature and fiction; general antiquarian books
OWNER: Bela Batta
SIZE: Large (70,000 used hardbacks, 30,000 used
paperbacks)
SPECIAL SERVICES: N/A
SPECIAL EVENTS: N/A
GETTING THERE: Royal York subway station, #76
or #15 bus south; parking on street

The Batta Book Store literally overflows with worthy
books, at prices so low that other dealers often obtain
their stock here. Hardcover books occupy the shelves,
with paperbacks at half price in the centre of the store.
A back room is arranged very compactly in stacks, and
on the floor below lies a catacomb of book-filled orange
crates. Categories include biography, business, fiction,
juvenile, literary criticism, literary biographies, literature, music, occult, philosophy, plays, poetry, science,
travel, etc. The store has particular strengths in Amer-
icana, Canadiana, first editions of literature, history
and politics, literary translations, mystery and detec-
tion, nature, and sexology. Everywhere I found books
I would be interested in reading: Proust's *Jean Santeuil*,
Irving's *The World According to Garp*, Thomas Berger's
Arthur Rex: A Legendary Novel. One should note the
unconventional hours: 2–7 p.m., Monday through
Saturday.

THE BEGUILING

601 Markham Street (in Markham
Village, near Bathurst and Bloor)
Toronto, Ontario M6G 2L7
416-533-9168 (FAX same)

SPECIALTY: Alternative comics and culture,
underground, new wave comic books, fiction,
non-fiction, and art books
OWNER: Steve Solomos and Sean Scoffield
SIZE: Medium
SPECIAL SERVICES: Reserve service, special orders,
search services
SPECIAL EVENTS: Cartoonists do signings, book
launchings, poetry and prose readings, comics
festivals at the Canadian National Exhibition
GETTING THERE: Bathurst subway station on the
Bloor line; limited street parking

The Beguiling specializes in alternative and underground comic books from the 1960s to the present.
In addition to the usual Marvel and DC superhero
comics, one finds a more literate selection of comics
than in most stores, including Japanese comics, political cartoons, work by Toronto artists, and collections
of contemporary syndicated comic strips as well as
classic newspaper comic strips in book form (e.g., Little
Orphan Annie, Terry and the Pirates, L'il Abner, and
Fearless Fosdick). The store also carries a certain number of books in art, photography, women's studies, and
general fiction and non-fiction.

BESTSELLERS

Eaton Centre, Dundas Court
(at Yonge Street)
P.O. Box 37
Toronto, Ontario M5G 1Z3
416-593-8857 (FAX same)

SPECIALTY: Popular books, CDs, and cassettes
OWNER: Individually owned stores
SIZE: Small
SPECIAL SERVICES: Special orders
SPECIAL EVENTS: Book signings; character
appearances by Tom & Jerry, Snoopy, Bugs Bunny,
etc.

Bestsellers, until recently a chain of nearly identical bookstores, has now become a series of individually owned stores, retaining the chain title but each with its own purchasing policy. Some have maintained the original format, selling the top twenty hardbacks, fiction and non-fiction, and the top twenty paperbacks, fiction and non-fiction (in other words, eighty titles), plus the top twenty CDs and, generally, a small selection of videos. Others, notably the branch at St. Clair Centre, have branched out into personal development videos, audio-books, and books appealing to the local neighbourhood. Retail locations in the Toronto area include Eaton Centre (416-593-8857), Commerce Court (416-360-1623), St. Clair Centre (416-927-0235, FAX 416-283-2198), North York City Centre (416-226-9844), Mutual Group Centre (416-236-9010), The Promenade (905-889-5224), and Hazelton Lanes (416-969-8731).

BOB MILLER BOOK ROOM

180 Bloor Street West
Lower Concourse
(near Avenue Road)
Toronto, Ontario M5S 2V6
416-922-3557 (FAX 416-922-4281)

SPECIALTY: Humanities and social sciences
OWNER: Carol Vine
SIZE: Large
SPECIAL SERVICES: Special orders, mail orders
SPECIAL EVENTS: N/A
GETTING THERE: Between Museum subway station
on the Spadina line and the St. George station on
the Bloor line; parking on street

What greater pleasure can there be for the serious bibliophile than to enter a really serious bookstore, particularly one as well laid out as the Bob Miller Book Room! The large floor area is divided by bookcases into a series of alcoves, separated by subject area, with new arrivals located in the shelves facing the centre of the store. Subject areas include African studies, Canadian literature, Caribbean and Latin American literature, child psychology, children, classics and philosophy, comparative religion, criticism, dictionaries, drama, economics, education, families and marriage, fiction, film studies, history (subdivided by country), Japanese literature, Judaica, Middle Eastern literature, music, native studies, Old and Middle English literature, poetry anthologies, political science, psychology, social sciences, systematic theology, women, and world religions.

THE BOOK BARREL

2284 Bloor Street West
Toronto, Ontario M6S 1N9
416-767-7417 (FAX 416-231-5417)

SPECIALTY: Quality literature and children's books
OWNER: Bill and Mike Doherty
SIZE: Small
SPECIAL SERVICES: Special orders (computer-based book search)
SPECIAL EVENTS: Storytelling for children
GETTING THERE: Runnymede subway station; public parking lot behind store

The Book Barrel is a neighbourhood bookstore devoted to the fine art of browsing. The books are separated by category, but there are no labels to identify them. Once having identified a section, the browser will be tantalized by intriguing titles not to be found in many other bookstores. At the time of my visit, the entertainment section included *All I Really Need to Know I Learned from Watching Star Trek*, *Round Up the Usual Suspects — The Making of Casablanca*, and *The I Hate Madonna Handbook*. Travel books included *Walt Disney World for Adults*, *Country Roads of Ontario*, and *Treehouse: The Art and Craft of Living Out on a Limb*. The owners buy books that interest them and that meet the needs of the neighbourhood, an area of Toronto with a European flavour. A separate room called "Kids' Books" has a sizeable collection, followed by a small back room of discount books.

BOOK CELLAR

1560 Yonge Street (near St. Clair)
Toronto, Ontario M4T 1Z7
416-967-5577 (No FAX)

SPECIALTY: General, best-sellers, magazines and periodicals, cards, remainders
OWNER: Cover to Cover, Inc.
SIZE: Medium
SPECIAL SERVICES: Special orders
SPECIAL EVENTS: Occasional author signings
GETTING THERE: St. Clair subway station; public parking behind store

The Book Cellar, up a short flight of stairs north of Yonge and St. Clair, offers an attractive, spacious area for buyers and browsers. Books are well-labelled and displayed in the centre of the store with shelves on the wall, including some 1,500 magazines. The store carries a general collection of books in biography, children, cooking, fiction, health, history, mystery, science fiction, and science, among others, with separate displays for new fiction, and staff recommendations. There is a large selection of remainders and bargain books; discounts are also offered on all current titles. The store is so aesthetically attractive, with carpeted floors, trade paperbacks displayed face out, and classical music in the background, that you hate to leave it.

THE BOOK CELLAR YORKVILLE

142 Yorkville Avenue
(near Avenue Road)
Toronto, Ontario M5R 1C2
416-925-9955 (FAX 416-925-0567)

SPECIALTY: General bookstore with strengths in travel and art
OWNER: Lori Bruner
SIZE: Medium
SPECIAL SERVICES: Mail orders, open seven days a week until 11 p.m. (midnight on weekends)
SPECIAL EVENTS: Artist signings, book launches
GETTING THERE: Bay subway station (Cumberland exit) on the Bloor line or Museum station on the Yonge line; parking lots at Avenue Road and Yorkville and at Cumberland and Bay

The Book Cellar Yorkville offers a wide assortment of fiction and non-fiction as well as a large selection of magazines and out-of-town newspapers. There is one whole wall of travel books and another of cookbooks, as well as a good-sized collection of biography and autobiography, sale books, children's books, coffee-table books, and books on tape.

BOOK CITY

501 Bloor Street West
(east of Bathurst)
Toronto, Ontario M5S 1Y2
416-961-4496 (FAX 416-961-9311)

SPECIALTY: General selection and remainders
OWNER: Frans Donker
SIZE: Large
SPECIAL SERVICES: Special orders
SPECIAL EVENTS: Book launches
GETTING THERE: Spadina subway station on Yonge or Bloor lines; parking on street

Fortunate are those who have Book City as their neighbourhood bookstore! The store directory lists 78 categories, from "Animals" to "Yoga," with a guide on where to find what you need. New hardcover books are discounted 10% and there is a nice collection of trade paperbacks as well as mass-market paperbacks. The quiet, well-illuminated store seems to go on and on. The mystery section keeps virtually *all* of an author's works, not just the most recent. Children's books occupy a neat nook of their own. A nearly complete run of "Everyman's Library" offers attractively bound, inexpensive editions of the classics. Three other branches may be found at 2350 Bloor Street West (416-766-9412), 1950 Queen Street East (416-698-1444), and 348 Danforth Avenue (416-469-9997). All four stores are "open late seven days a week."

THE BOOK COMPANY

BCE Place, 181 Bay Street
(between Front and Wellington)
Toronto, Ontario M5J 2T3
416-601-1847 (FAX 416-601-1849)

SPECIALTY: General collection, upscale, many art
books, trade paperbacks
OWNER: Chapters Inc. Head Office, 90 Ronson
Drive, Rexdale, Ontario, M9W 1C1
SIZE: Medium (30,000 titles)
SPECIAL SERVICES: Special orders
SPECIAL EVENTS: Author signings, series of readings
GETTING THERE: Union station on Yonge subway
line; nearby municipal parking

This is one of the most beautiful bookstores in the city:
a marble floor surrounds the central carpeted area;
globe lamps and recessed lighting shine on neatly displayed section labels. Despite the number of books, the
store gives a feeling of space, and many of the books
have their covers facing out. There are large sections
in biography, Canadiana, children's books, cooking,
fiction, history, literature, mystery, performing arts,
sociology, and travel, with many smaller sections
such as crafts, lifestyle, health, home, and art. Other
locations include 1470 Yonge Street (416-928-1550),
First Canadian Place (416-869-1079), and Sherway
Gardens (416-620-4997).

BOOK FACTORY, INC.
(a.k.a. GIANT BOOK SALE)

105 McCaul (between Queen and Dundas)
Toronto, Ontario M5T 2W7
416-599-4545 (No FAX)

SPECIALTY: Publishers' overstock
OWNER: Lieu Ngugyn
SIZE: Medium
SPECIAL SERVICES: Special orders
SPECIAL EVENTS: N/A
GETTING THERE: Dundas streetcar; parking on
street

The two large high-ceilinged rooms filled with book-
covered tables give the impression of a cross between a
warehouse and a flea market. Don't let appearances
deceive you: all the books are new and heavily discounted. In contrast to bookstores whose remainder
books, unsorted, occupy a single corner, Book Factory,
which also goes by the name of Giant Book Sale,
helpfully separates the publisher's overstock into
categories: biography, business, child care, children,
computers, cookbooks, crafts, decorating, fiction,
games, hardcover novels, health and beauty, history,
housecare and woodworking, humour and comics,
literature, nature and pets, New Age, photography,
poetry, religion, science, self-help and diets, and travel.
Many worthy books appear among the forgotten or
forgettable.

BOOK MARK

2964 Bloor Street West
(at Jackson Avenue)
Toronto, Ontario M8X 1B7
416-233-2191 (FAX 416-233-2192)

SPECIALTY: General
OWNER: Sue Houghting and Dave Eustace
SIZE: Medium (20,000 titles)
SPECIAL SERVICES: Special orders, giftwrap
SPECIAL EVENTS: Author readings and signings
GETTING THERE: Royal York subway station;
   parking in back

Book Mark recently moved from a converted apartment into a modern bookstore, whose green walls provide a calm backdrop for brass rubbings, a rocking horse, and other decorations from the former establishment. Wooden bookcases set at an angle give a sense of individual alcoves for books on art, biography, adult and children's literature, cooking, history, travel, and general non-fiction. While one can find popular mysteries, romances, and science fiction, the overall impression of the store is that of a collection of very well-chosen books. A quotation from Erasmus mounted on the wall behind the cash register reads, "When I get a little money, I buy books, and if any is left, I buy food and clothes."

BOOKLAND

350 Queen Street East
(near Parliament)
Toronto, Ontario M5A 1T1
416-363-4820 (No FAX)

SPECIALTY: Used books, autographs, movie star ads
   and photos, large selection of vintage magazines,
   1910 to present
OWNER: Joe Sandner
SIZE: Medium
SPECIAL SERVICES: Search service for movie
   memorabilia
SPECIAL EVENTS: N/A
GETTING THERE: Queen Street streetcar; parking
   on street

Bookland, an unprepossessing store from the outside, contains a great number of books in a deceptively small space. The stock is well organized in clearly marked sections. Owner Joe Sandner observes, "It's not a bookstore anymore — now I'm just recycling paper." One finds used books in most of the usual categories from American history to women's studies. The store's major emphasis is on films, with biographies of movie stars, books on filmmaking, movie star ads, photos, and movie magazines.

THE BOOKMAN TEXTBOOK & EDUCATIONAL OUTLET

4910 Yonge Street
(side door, lower level, three
streets north of Sheppard)
North York, Ontario M2N 5N5
416-224-5300 (FAX 416-224-5324)

SPECIALTY: School textbooks (kindergarten to OAC,
university, and ESL)
OWNER: Corporation
SIZE: Medium
SPECIAL SERVICES: Mail textbooks, K–13
SPECIAL EVENTS: N/A
GETTING THERE: Sheppard subway station on the
Yonge line; parking lot east of Yonge

The Bookman carries all textbooks used in private,
public, and parochial schools in Ontario. Books are
arranged by grade level, with texts in Canadian history,
English, mathematics, reading and writing, science,
social studies, and spelling. The store also carries
teacher materials, workbooks, educational games, ESL
materials, and five bookcases of novels, plays, short
stories and literature in paperback editions.

BOOKS AND GIFTS OF LIGHT AND USUI REIKI CENTRE

3261 Bayview Avenue
(north of Finch)
Toronto, Ontario M2K 1G4
416-229-0503 (FAX 416-590-0238)

SPECIALTY: Personal growth and self development
OWNER: Sue MacKay and Ellen Rose
SIZE: Small
SPECIAL SERVICES: Special orders
SPECIAL EVENTS: Classes and workshops on reiki,
yoga, miracles, aikido
GETTING THERE: Finch subway station, Cummer
bus; parking in mall at 3311 Bayview

Reiki is a Japanese term which means "universal life
energy," the energy that lives in all creation. Reiki is
also used to describe a natural method of healing. The
bookstore supports the activities of the Reiki Centre
and includes books in a number of categories: angels,
channelling, children, cookbooks, death and dying,
divination, fiction, healing, inspirational, native, and
personal growth. The store also carries cards, candles,
crystals, cassettes, CDs of New Age music, incense
sticks, and tea. A second room displays the peculiarly
magical artwork of native artist David Johnson. The
centre issues a newsletter, *Lightlines*, six times a year.

BOOKS AND MUSIC PLUS

711 Mount Pleasant Avenue
(just south of Eglinton)
Toronto, Ontario M4S 2N4
416-440-1386 (NO FAX)

SPECIALTY: Quality CDs, tapes, records, books
  purchased, sold, and traded
OWNER: Norman Boroumand
SIZE: Small
SPECIAL SERVICES: N/A
SPECIAL EVENTS: N/A
GETTING THERE: Eglinton subway station, then
  Eglinton bus; parking at rear of store

Behind the counter of Books and Music Plus, a sign reads, "What is worth doing at all is worth doing well," a motto which summarizes the philosophy of this bookstore. Though customers constantly bring in used books, very few end up on the shelves. The rest end up in a bin outside the store marked "Free," in which I discovered, during my visit, a hard-cover copy of *Portnoy's Complaint* and a book of speeches by Robertson Davies. On the shelves one finds reasonably priced, fairly recent used books in very good condition, largely hardcover, in the fields of art, biography, history, literature, New Age, occult, philosophy, poetry, psychology, religion, sociology, spirituality, and women's studies. The store also carries used CDs and cassettes in jazz, blues, and classic rock. A second branch of the store is located at 101 Dundas Street East (at Church).

BOOKS FOR BUSINESS

120 Adelaide Street West
(between Bay and York)
Toronto, Ontario M5H 1T1
416-362-7822 or 1-800-668-9372
(FAX 416-362-9795)
e-mail: info@booksforbusiness.on.ca

SPECIALTY: Business books
OWNER: Jane Cooney
SIZE: Small (9,000 to 10,000 volumes)
SPECIAL SERVICES: Research projects,
  international mail orders, market studies
SPECIAL EVENTS: Book launches
GETTING THERE: King or St. Andrew subway
  station; underground parking lots in area; no
  parking on street

In the heart of Toronto's business district lies a bookstore devoted to business. As Jane Cooney explains in the store's 1995 catalogue, "When most people think of Canadian book publishing and writing, the names Margaret Atwood and Robertson Davies are more likely to spring to mind than, say, David Crane, Michael Bliss, or Walter Stewart. Nevertheless, writing about business is an important part of our writing establishment." Here you will find, attractively displayed in dark wood bookcases, works on accounting, biography, communications, computers, current affairs, economics and statistics, education, finance, financial markets, human resources, industries, international business, investment management, management, motivation and methods, personal finance, reference, sales and marketing, small business, taxes, and technology. The store also issues a free quarterly newsletter containing updated lists of new business books, an annual catalogue of Canadian business titles, and specialized bibliographies on business topics.

THE BOOKSMITH

2012B Queen Street East
(near Woodbine)
Toronto, Ontario M4L 1J3
416-698-4768 (No FAX)

SPECIALTY: General bookstore specializing in magazines
OWNER: Rosaire Langlois
SIZE: Small
SPECIAL SERVICES: Special orders
SPECIAL EVENTS: N/A
GETTING THERE: Queen Street streetcar; parking on side streets

The Booksmith virtually overflows with books: there are piles of books on the floor, books in front of other books on the shelves. The collection consists primarily of paperback books on art, astrology, babies, biography, health, history, mystery, reference, women, and science fiction, with a few trade paperbacks on literature and a number of signed copies. The store features more than 500 magazines. The children's collection includes youth books and romances in series. The collection, though small, contains many good choices of books.

CCH CANADIAN LIMITED

6 Garamond Court
(near Don Mills and Wynford)
Toronto, Ontario M3C 1Z5
416-441-2992 (FAX 416-444-9011)

SPECIALTY: Tax books
OWNER: Private corporation
SIZE: Small
SPECIAL SERVICES: Loose-leaf services, Canada tax guides
SPECIAL EVENTS: N/A
GETTING THERE: Don Mills bus from Pape subway station; parking on premises

CCH Canadian develops products that "navigate professionals through the regulator waters, national and international, of business and tax law" and supply "practical information on emerging export markets." CCH Canadian offers software and CD-ROM products, international information, subscription services, bound books, newsletters, and professional development seminars. The catalogue gives detailed descriptions of books and services in accounting and taxation, business, human resources, legal matters, professional development, and products in French. A small display area contains samples of recent publications, but the firm operates primarily as a mail-order business.

CMG BOOKS & ART
CHARLES MUS GALLERY

156 Davenport Road
(between Avenue Road and Bay)
Toronto, Ontario M5R 1J2
416-921-5870 (FAX 416-921-6296)

SPECIALTY: Books on the arts of Africa, Oceania, Pre-Columbia, and First peoples of North America (including Inuit); general art books
OWNER: Charles Mus
SIZE: Small (2,000 on arts of Africa; 4,500 titles in all)
SPECIAL SERVICES: Mail orders
SPECIAL EVENTS: N/A
GETTING THERE: Rosedale subway station on Yonge line; Bay station on Bloor line; parking on street

The Charles Mus Gallery is located in an interesting neighbourhood full of art galleries, law offices, photography studios, Persian rug dealers, interior decorating consultants, haute couture salons, wine boutiques, shirtmakers, and a cat doctor. One first enters an all-white room displaying African masks and sculptures. The book collection proper lies in a second room, quite dark, with spotlights and floodlights providing a rather dramatic illumination. Atop the bookcases are a collection of African neckrests, still used by some to maintain their elaborate coiffures during the night. The collection includes general books on sub-Saharan Africa as well as African art (crafts, masks, sculpture, textiles), general tribal art, oceanic art (e.g., *The Art of Easter Island*), African-American art, Pre-Columbian, Inuit, and North American Indian art. A catalogue lists all the titles carried by the store, which carries on an international mail-order business in addition to the retail store and gallery.

CANADIAN PROFESSIONAL
INFORMATION CENTRE LTD.

6200 Dixie Road, Unit 108
Mississauga, Ontario L5T 2E1
905-670-1250 (FAX 905-670-1252)

SPECIALTY: Computer, engineering, business, manufacturing, and medical
OWNER: Jim Arnold
SIZE: Small (1,500 titles in stock and 1.5 m available)
SPECIAL SERVICES: Special orders, mail orders (constitutes the bulk of the business)
SPECIAL EVENTS: Will display at seminars and conferences; bi-monthly catalogue
GETTING THERE: Mississauga Transit, one kilometre north of highway 401 on Dixie Road; parking on premises

The Canadian Professional Information Centre is a professional/technical bookstore that caters to consultants, teachers, students, corporations, and libraries. CPIC is the official bookstore for The Purchasing Management Association of Canada, The Material Management Institute, The Society of Manufacturing Engineers, and others. You can shop in person or call and request a catalogue of technical books. The bi-monthly catalogues contain brief descriptions of books in project management, quality control, software, instruments and controls, electronics and electrical engineering, maintenance and industrial, stress and failures, manufacturing and design, mechanical and industrial engineering, plastics and ceramics, metals and manufacturing handbooks, environmental and chemical engineering, construction, and civil engineering. The firm serves as distributor for two engineering societies in the U.S., publishes books and videos, and sells home study courses.

CAVERSHAM BOOKSELLERS

98 Harbord Street
(at Spadina)
Toronto, Ontario M5S 1G6
416-944-0962 (FAX 416-944-0963)

SPECIALTY: Psychoanalysis, psychotherapy, psychiatry, psychology
OWNER: Peter Heyworth and Christine Dunbar
SIZE: Small (7,000 titles)
SPECIAL SERVICES: Special orders, mail orders, conferences, course orders, library orders
SPECIAL EVENTS: N/A
GETTING THERE: Wellesley bus or Spadina subway station; parking on street

Caversham Booksellers serves a professional clientele of psychologists, psychiatrists and social workers by providing a serious collection of works on psychology and related topics, including abuse, addiction, art therapy, brief psychotherapy, cognitive psychology, developmental psychology, gestalt, infant, child and adolescent studies, Jungian psychology, marital and family studies, older age, sexuality, transcultural studies, women's studies, and men's studies. A large, well-informed staff is happy to provide assistance. Founded in 1989, the bookstore continues to grow, and has extended its boundaries to displays and sales at professional conferences.

CHAMPLAIN BOOK STORE (LIBRAIRIE CHAMPLAIN)

468 Queen Street East (near Parliament)
Toronto, Ontario M5A 1T7
416-364-4345 (FAX 416-364-8843)

SPECIALTY: French books, magazines, cassettes, videos, software, greeting cards
OWNER: Privately owned
SIZE: Large
SPECIAL SERVICES: Special orders, mail orders
SPECIAL EVENTS: Author signings
GETTING THERE: Queen Street streetcar; free parking behind the store

Champlain Book Store is a large and lively store serving Toronto's francophone community, government, translators, and schools with French-language material from France, Belgium, and Québec. Overhead signs in the form of giant clouds, each with a logo or illustration, indicate general areas: *histoire, arts et loisirs, fiction, enseignement, sciences, jeunesse, dictionnaires, littérature/classique*. Individual subsections are indicated at the top of each bookcase. *Fiction*, for example, is subdivided into *romans canadiens, contes — nouvelles, science fiction, adolescents*, and *romans français*. *Jeunesse* is subdivided into *canadiens, enfants, théâtre jeunesse, essais littéraire et scientifique*, and *jeux educatifs*. Large paperback collections are kept intact — for example, the "J'ai lu" and "Que sais-je?" series. French-language videos include both translations (Disney's "Le roi lion" and "Alice au pays des merveilles") and original French material (e.g., "Astérix"). The section of children's books similarly includes French translations of all of Robert Munsch's books in addition to original French-language storybooks.

CHAN SHEUNG KEE BOOK CO.

463 Dundas Street West,
lower level (near Spadina)
Toronto, Ontario M5T 1G8
416-596-7709 (FAX 416-596-7432)

SPECIALTY: Chinese books
OWNER: Kelvin Chan
SIZE: Small
SPECIAL SERVICES: N/A
SPECIAL EVENTS: N/A
GETTING THERE: Dundas Street streetcar; parking on street

Toronto's Chinatown has been described as looking very much like Hong Kong in the 1950s and 60s, and many of the books in the area bookstores are holdovers from an earlier era. The Chan Sheung Kee Book Company sells some very old books on child care, an ancient *Dictionary of Radio Technology* in Japanese, English, and Chinese, but it also has more up-to-date books than most of the other Chinese bookstores. You will find recent computer books, Chinese translations of Calvin and Hobbes, new opera librettos, and novelizations of recent movies as well as books on ancient and modern literature, biography, business (mostly of the "how to get rich" variety), child care, cookbooks (both English and Chinese), fortune-telling, health, interior design, legendary literature, photography, and psychology. The store also carries books on Qui Gong, a special science of the human body regarded as an alternative to traditional medicine.

CHAPTERS
Opening soon at 110 Bloor Street and at Yonge and Steeles

See description of Burlington store in section on Out-of-Town Bookstores (page 159).

CHAPTERS BOOKSHOP

834 Yonge Street
(½ block north of Bloor)
Toronto, Ontario M4W 2H1
416-975-4370 (No FAX)

SPECIALTY: Rare and used books
OWNER: Frank Velikonja
SIZE: Medium
SPECIAL SERVICES: N/A
SPECIAL EVENTS: N/A
GETTING THERE: Bloor and Yonge subway staiton; parking on street

Chapters Bookshop, established before the Chapters bookstores born of the merger of Coles and Smith-Books, presents a striking appearance, with light pine shelves extending like library stacks several hundred feet deep into the store. This impressive collection of used books includes adventure, Africa, American, anthropology, art, Canada (a large section), Canadian literature, chess, cooking, exploration, fiction, history, Holocaust, Judaica, linguistics, literary criticism, mystery, mythology, occult and New Age, oriental philosophy, philosophy, plays, poetry, political science, psychology, reference, religion, science, science fiction and fantasy, sociology, and war history. Recent hardcover books in good condition sell for roughly half the original price (e.g., Ann Beattie's *What Was Mine* for $13.95 instead of $26.50; John Updike's *The Afterlife*, published in 1994 at $32 sells here for $19). The collection is still growing, but the choices so far show a discriminating taste.

CHILDREN'S BOOK STORE

2532 Yonge Street (near St. Clements, 6 blocks north of Eglinton)
Toronto, Ontario M4P 2H7
416-480-0233 (FAX 416-480-9345)

SPECIALTY: Children's books, audiotapes, videos, and CD-ROMS
OWNER: Judy and Hy Sarick
SIZE: Medium (30,000 titles)
SPECIAL SERVICES: Institutional sales to schools and libraries
SPECIAL EVENTS: Occasional author visits; special activities in the fall and during March break
GETTING THERE: Eglinton subway station, Yonge #97 bus; municipal parking lot one block south

The Children's Book Store, Toronto's oldest children's bookstore, offers books, audio, and video for children from birth to age sixteen. The large collection is arranged into interesting categories: about children and their books, audio-video, beginning readers, cars, planes and things, fiction for older readers, first novels, French language books, mind and body, Mother Goose (an entire section of around forty titles), picture books, poetry, reference/arts, social studies/science, things to do, traditional tales. There is also a section of "staff picks." The Children's Book Store has recently added a selection of CD-ROMS for children and youth as well as viewing stations for CD-ROM titles. The store is wheelchair and stroller accessible.

CHILDREN'S FRENCH STORE

1486 Danforth Avenue (near Coxwell)
Toronto, Ontario M4J 1N4
416-465-3015 (FAX same)

SPECIALTY: Children's books in French
OWNER: Marilyn Banack
SIZE: Small
SPECIAL SERVICES: Special orders
SPECIAL EVENTS: Artists and storytellers
GETTING THERE: Coxwell subway station on the
  Bloor line; parking on street

Marilyn Banack, a former French-as-a-second-language teacher, runs a bookstore catering to parents and teachers of children in French-immersion programs and to school librarians. The collection is not large, but the store specializes in expert advice. Ms. Banack listens to kids read, then recommends books to their parents. She supplies teachers with stories, posters, marionettes, T-shirts ("Le français, c'est fantastique"), buttons, cassette tapes, and other teaching materials including "Fun Plays for French Second-Language Students." The store is decorated with stuffed animals, maps, posters, paintings, puppets, and a giant rainbow over the counter.

CHINA BOOK STORE

523 Gerrard Street East
(near Broadview)
Toronto, Ontario M4M 1Y2
416-469-2110 (FAX 416-462-3852)

SPECIALTY: Chinese books and videos
OWNER: William Chui
SIZE: Small
SPECIAL SERVICES: Special orders
SPECIAL EVENTS: Sell tickets to Chinese shows
  (agents for Chinese singers appearing at Roy
  Thompson Hall)
GETTING THERE: Broadview subway station on
  Bloor line, then streetcar south; parking on street
  or at public lot

The China Book Store occupies a single room, half of which is given over to rental videocassettes, including both language instruction and hundreds of Chinese films. The books turn over at a slower rate than the videos, which explains the presence of quite obsolete computer manuals and economics books, some in English translation (e.g., *A Concise History of Chinese Economic Thought*). Other categories of books include Chinese novels, cookbooks, fortune-telling (palmistry), health, hobbies, music, science fiction, sports, and travel. The store also sells cassette tapes for learning English and a variety of dictionaries, including English/Vietnamese, English/Mandarin, English/Chinese, Chinese/Chinese, medical dictionaries, and dictionaries of idioms and phrases.

CHRISTIAN BOOK AND GIFT CENTRE

714 Bloor Street West
(near Christie)
Toronto, Ontario M6G 1L4
416-535-1920 (No FAX)

SPECIALTY: Korean books
OWNER: Meung Joon Kim
SIZE: Small
SPECIAL SERVICES: N/A
SPECIAL EVENTS: N/A
GETTING THERE: Bloor subway to Christie station; parking on street

The Christian Book and Gift Centre is one of a number of neighbourhood bookstores serving Toronto's international community. While there are a few books in English, the collection consists primarily of Korean-language books, notably Bibles (English, Korean, and bilingual), cookbooks (several in English, including *Traditional Korean Cooking* and *Healthful Korean Cooking*), Bible stories for children, children's books, devotional guides, dictionaries, hymnals, and novels. The store also carries Korean versions of recent computer manuals. One may also find cassettes and CDs of Korean music.

CHRISTIAN BOOK ROOM

338B Pape Avenue
(at Gerrard)
Toronto, Ontario M4M 2W7
416-469-0067 (No FAX)

SPECIALTY: Family books for all ages
OWNER: Mrs. Rees
SIZE: Small
SPECIAL SERVICES: N/A
SPECIAL EVENTS: N/A
GETTING THERE: College/Carleton streetcar; parking on street

The Christian Book Room is a small, single-room store with an emphasis on personal religion as opposed to theology. Posters in the store window proclaim "We Have a Friend in Jesus," "Jesus Is Lord" and "Jesus ♥ You." The collection includes Bibles in many languages, children's books, religious aids such as atlases and dictionaries, greeting cards, devotional guides, and posters with uplifting messages.

CIVIC GARDEN CENTRE TRELLIS SHOP

777 Lawrence Avenue East
(at Edwards Gardens)
Toronto, Ontario M3C IP2
416-397-1359 (FAX 416-397-1354)

SPECIALTY: Gardening and horticulture
OWNER: City of Toronto
SIZE: Small
SPECIAL SERVICES: Mail orders, special orders
SPECIAL EVENTS: Workshops, classes, lectures and special programs, plant sales
GETTING THERE: Leslie or Lawrence bus from Eglinton subway station; parking at Edwards Gardens

The white trellis, artificial flowers, and arbour of the Trellis Shop make you feel as if you've strayed into an unexpected corner of a garden, an illusion enhanced by background recordings of nature sounds. The store offers books on virtually every aspect of gardening: alpine and rock gardens, birds, bromeliads, bulbs, cacti, container gardens, cookbooks, drawing and painting, edible and wild mushrooms, ferns, flower arranging, garden flowers, gardening under glass, gardens of the world, general gardening, ground covers and lawns, herbs, indoor gardening, landscape gardening, lawns, nature, orchids, organic gardening, perennials, pests and diseases, Peterson's field guides, propagation, pruning, roses, sale books, Taylor's guides, vegetables, water gardening, and wildflowers. In addition to the Trellis Shop, the Civic Garden Centre supports a library covering all aspects of gardening, horticulture, history, and floral arts. The centre also sponsors workshops, classes, lectures and special programs, publishes the *Trellis* newsletter, organizes plant sales, Master Gardeners' activities and garden tours, and maintains a gardening information hotline.

CLASCOM COMPUTERS

90 Adelaide Street West
(at Sheppard St.)
Toronto, Ontario M5H 3V9
416-369-9944 (FAX 416-369-9786)

SPECIALTY: Computer and business books
OWNER: Vincent Chan
SIZE: Small
SPECIAL SERVICES: Special orders, institutional sales
SPECIAL EVENTS: Booths at shows
GETTING THERE: King, Queen, St. Patrick or St. Andrew subway stations; parking lot on Sheppard St. or at City Hall

Clascom Computers serves computer professionals in Toronto's business district as well as computer company and bank libraries with a well-organized stock of technical books on algorithms and numerical methods, business, computer programming languages, computer architecture, the Internet, networking and communications, object-oriented technology and languages, operating systems, as well as two dozen computer journals. In addition to book sales, which constitute only 5% of the business, Clascom Computers supplies hardware and software to banks and large businesses in the area. A quarterly newsletter lists coming events and offers reviews of new books, hardware and software. Outside the store, bicycle messengers in skin-tight suits and aerodynamic helmets whiz by at the speed of e-mail daemons.

COLES
THE BOOK PEOPLE

Chapters Inc. Head Office,
90 Ronson Drive
Rexdale, Ontario M9W 1C1
416-243-3138 (FAX 416-243-8964)

SPECIALTY: General
OWNER: Chapters Inc.
SIZE: Medium
SPECIAL SERVICES: Special orders
SPECIAL EVENTS: N/A

Coles, perhaps the best known of bookstore chains, offers great quantities of books in functional surroundings. One can find current titles on a variety of subjects, from biography and business to sports and travel, with books for young readers as well as adults. The chain's claim that "There's a Coles Near You" would seem to apply to most of Toronto's inhabitants, for there are outlets at Centrepoint, Commerce Court, Don Mills Shopping Centre, East York Town Centre, Fairview Mall, Toronto Eaton Centre, and the Yorkdale Shopping Centre. Additional stores may be found in Agincourt (Woodside Square), Etobicoke (Sherway Gardens), and Scarborough (Cedarbrae Mall, Eglinton Square, Malvern Town Centre, Morningside Mall). See the separate entry for the World's Biggest Bookstore, at 20 Edward Street. Coles and SmithBooks have now merged into Chapters Inc., which also owns Chapters Bookstores, Active Minds, and The Book Company.

COLLEGE BOOKSTORE AND
MR REPRESENTATIONS

534 College Street
(between Bathurst and Euclid)
Toronto, Ontario M6G 1A6
416-960-3731 (FAX 416-960-9811)

SPECIALTY: Portuguese books, general
OWNER: Maria Rodrigues
SIZE: Small
SPECIAL SERVICES: N/A
SPECIAL EVENTS: N/A
GETTING THERE: Bathurst subway station; parking behind store

The College Bookstore serves as a neighbourhood bookstore for the city's Portuguese community and supplies primary schools, high schools, and libraries. The store sells French, English, Spanish, and Portuguese dictionaries as well as Portuguese-language art books, children's books, cookbooks, crafts and gardening books, fiction, gift books, history books, maps, meditation aids, and poetry. There are dime novels and Portuguese translations of English best-sellers, such as Robert Ludlum's *O Manuscrito Chancellor*. There are a few magazines and newspapers, mostly from Portugal, but some from Brazil.

THE COMIC EMPORIUM, INC.

6 Edward Street
(near Yonge and Dundas)
Toronto, Ontario M5G 1C9
416-597-9405 (No FAX)

SPECIALTY: New comic books
OWNER: Andrew Lee
SIZE: Small
SPECIAL SERVICES: Subscription service
SPECIAL EVENTS: N/A
GETTING THERE: One block north of Dundas subway station on Yonge line; parking on street

Located two doors down from the World's Biggest Bookstore is one of the city's smaller and best-organized comic-book stores, The Comic Emporium. The owner believes that things have to be easy to find and attractive to customers, so new issues are displayed with full covers facing out, and are separated by publisher (Marvel, Image, DC, Dark Horse, Viz, and a miscellaneous section including Disney comics, Simpsons, Archie, and others). All comics are bagged and boarded so that they remain in mint condition for discriminating collectors. The Comic Emporium carries over 300 different titles every month, including a number of small presses as well as mainstream comics. The bins in the centre of the store offer a variety of back issues of series such as *Spiderman*, *Batman*, *Shi*, and *Strangers in Paradise*. The store also sells Magic (a role-playing game with cards), non-sport cards, graphic novels, and a selection of Japanese animation videos.

COMIC PRINCE BOOKSTORE

5694 Highway 7 (one traffic light
west of Markham Road)
Markham, Ontario L3P 1B4
905-294-6178 (No FAX)

SPECIALTY: Comic books
OWNER: Gary Supp
SIZE: Medium
SPECIAL SERVICES: N/A
SPECIAL EVENTS: N/A
GETTING THERE: Parking in shopping plaza

Comic Prince Bookstore offers a large variety of main-line comics including some not regularly encountered in the smaller stores. Under "S" I found *Savage Dragon*, *Scout*, *Secret Defenders*, *Secret Origins*, *Secret Wars*, *Sgt. Fury*, *Sgt. Rock*, *Shadow States*, *Sherlock Holmes*, *Shi*, *Showcase*, *Speed Racer*, *Spirits of Revenge*, *Spring-Heel Jack*, *Star Brand*, *Static*, *Steed and Mrs. Peel*, *Steel*, *Strangers*, *Strikeforce Morituri*, *Strykeforce*, and *Suicide Squad*. Large format, hardcover, and graphic novels occupy an entire wall of the shop, which also sells figurines and some three dozen books on gaming. There are also collectors' editions of *Donald Duck*, *L'il Abner*, *Tintin*, and *Dr. Who*.

THE CONSTANT READER

111 Harbord Street
(near Spadina)
Toronto, Ontario M5S 1G7
416-972-0661 (No FAX)

SPECIALTY: New, used, and antiquarian books for children
OWNER: Private
SIZE: Small (8,000 titles)
SPECIAL SERVICES: Special orders, book searches, mail orders
SPECIAL EVENTS: N/A
GETTING THERE: Spadina subway station; parking on street

The Constant Reader occupies a distinctive niche on Harbord Street, where a number of fine bookstores cluster conveniently. This lovely small store has white lace curtains, brass lamps, and wooden shelves. During our visit, the bookstore owner was giving one youngster a quiet lesson in how to turn pages without bending the corners. The collection includes anthologies, art, biographies for children, classics, fairy tales and folktales, multicultural literature, music and poetry, with a small antiquarian section.

CONTACT EDITIONS, INC.

2289 Yonge Street
(near Eglinton)
Toronto, Ontario M4P 2E6
416-322-0777 (FAX 416-322-3226)

SPECIALTY: General bookstore with strengths in travel, psychology, modern art, and fiction
OWNER: Wesley Begg
SIZE: Medium (20,000 new; 10,000 used)
SPECIAL SERVICES: Special orders
SPECIAL EVENTS: Occasional half-price sale
GETTING THERE: Eglinton subway station on Yonge line; municipal lot one block away; metered parking on street

Contact Editions is an impressive bookstore with a strong collection of both new and used books. The first floor begins with three sections — New, Newer, and Newest — opposite a shelf of signed copies of books. Further into the store one finds new books in biography, business, children, fiction, food and drink, history, humour, language, literature, mystery (three bookcases), nature, performing arts, philosophy, poetry, reference, religion, science fiction, sports, The Mind (followed by The Body), travel, and young adult. The used and rare books are located on the second floor, past a suit of armour on the landing, and include modern first editions, art, belles lettres, cinema, history (ancient, Canadian, European, military), literary biography, travel and adventure, and mysteries and thrillers (a 1951 edition of Rex Stout's *Curtains for Three* sells for $75).

THE COOKBOOK STORE

850 Yonge Street (at Yorkville)
Toronto, Ontario M4W 2H1
416-920-2665 (FAX 416-920-3271)
Canada & U.S. 1-800-268-6018
e-mail: cooking@io.org
http://www.cook-book.com

SPECIALTY: Cookbooks, wine books, food and wine magazines
OWNER: Barbara Caffery and Josh Josephson
SIZE: Small (6,000 titles in stock)
SPECIAL SERVICES: Mail orders
SPECIAL EVENTS: Wine tastings, author signings, newsletter
GETTING THERE: Bloor & Yonge subway station; municipal parking lot one block away

The Cookbook Store, one of Toronto's best-known specialty bookstores, has hosted visits from many celebrities of the cooking field. The knowledgeable staff fields requests for advice from professional chefs or from amateur cooks. The casual visitor who may have wondered how there could be an entire bookstore devoted to cooking will be intrigued by titles such as *The Children's Birthday Cake Book*, *Are You Hungry Tonight — Elvis' Favorite Recipes*, *The Tuna Fish Gourmet*, *The Hungry Hiker's Book of Good Cooking*, *Blue Collar Food*, *A World of Curries*, *500 Fat-Free Recipes*, *Practical Thai Cooking*, and *Death by Chocolate*. In addition to books on Canadian, international, and vegetarian cooking, desserts, general reference, health and nutrition, and wines, the store also offers aprons, posters, and an assortment of culinary magazines. *Foodworks*, The Cookbook Store newsletter, provides capsule descriptions of dozens of books in various categories as well as a schedule of visiting authors. Readers with Internet access may wish to view the store's web site.

CRAZY CARLO COMICS AND GAMES

6 Belsize Drive
(near Yonge and Davisville)
Toronto, Ontario M4S 1L8
416-489-4429 (No FAX)

SPECIALTY: Mainline comics
OWNER: Carlo Pileggi
SIZE: Medium
SPECIAL SERVICES: Reserves comics for regular customers, special order games
SPECIAL EVENTS: N/A
GETTING THERE: Davisville subway station; parking on street

Carlo Pileggi likes to maintain a one-to-one relationship with his clients, learning their preferences, setting aside issues for collectors, and offering discount incentives for regular customers. (Members receive discounts of 15–30% off latest issues, 5–20% off back issues.) The store carries primarily mainline comics. Under "S," I found all the standards plus *Sandman Mystery Theater*, *Simpsons*, *Samurai*, *Sanctuary*, *Scarlett*, *Shadows Fall*, *Shatter*, and *Sin City*. An old issue of *The Flash*, originally selling for 10¢, now sells for $60. The store also rents Japanese animation videos and sells gaming products and a few science fiction books.

D. & E. LAKE, LTD.

239 King Street East
(near Sherbourne)
Toronto, Ontario M5A 1J9
416-863-9930 (FAX 416-863-9443)

SPECIALTY: Art and decorative arts, rare books, Canadiana, travel and illustrated books, maps and prints before 1900

OWNER: Donald Lake

SIZE: Large

SPECIAL SERVICES: N/A

SPECIAL EVENTS: N/A

GETTING THERE: Sherbourne bus or King streetcar; parking at two nearby lots

D. & E. Lake, Ltd. occupies three floors of an attractive Victorian building which includes a general shop and display area, a print and map gallery, an antiquarian book room and walk-in vault, a reference library, and a gallery. A brochure describes their inventory: rare books published before 1800 in all fields (incunabula, early printing, illustrated books, Canadiana-Americana, travel and topography, science, medicine, natural history, philosophy, political economy, law, British and European history and literature, classics and theology, art and architecture, cookery, bibliography); modern reference books on art, decorative arts and antiques (including carpets, ceramics, clocks, costumes, dolls, gold and silversmiths, jewelry, porcelain, glass, tapestry, textiles, toys, and woodworking), bibliography, and cartography; antique maps before 1850; antique prints before 1880; 18th- and 19th-century watercolours, drawings, and oil paintings; and autograph letters, documents and manuscripts, specializing in Canadiana. The books, new and used, occupy tall, decorated but unlabelled wooden bookcases, for this is not a browser's bookstore. The store issues numerous catalogues and bulletins.

DEC BOOKROOM

836 Bloor Street West
(two blocks east of Ossington)
Toronto, Ontario M6G 1M2
416-516-2966 (FAX 416-517-2967)

SPECIALTY: Alternative, hard-to-find books on anti-racism, development, environment, labour, peace and disarmament, politics, Third World, women's movement

OWNER: Development Education Centre

SIZE: Small

SPECIAL SERVICES: N/A

SPECIAL EVENTS: Serves as a meeting place for many in the leftist communities

GETTING THERE: Ossington subway station on the Bloor line; parking on street

The Development Education Centre (DEC), according to the *DEC News*, is a "diverse global education centre whose mandate is public education focusing on current global struggles for change. DEC works to foster links between Canadians and the peoples of Africa, Asia, the Middle East, Latin America and the Caribbean. DEC helps to identify ways Canadians can act in mutual solidarity and forge common links with those in the so-called Third World." The DEC Bookroom offers alternative books on Africa, anti-racism, Black history, children, education, environment, Europe, First Nations, gays/lesbians, health, labour, Latin America, media/culture, Middle East, organizing, peace/disarmament, political and social theory, South America, Third World, women (three bookcases), young people, and a section of *Libros en español*.

DRB MOTORS, INC.

168 Davenport Road
(between Bay and Avenue)
Toronto, Ontario M5R 1J2
416-922-8860 or 1-800-665-2665
(FAX 416-922-5937)
e-mail: drb@godin.on.ca

SPECIALTY: Transport titles: automobiles, motorcycles, trains, boats, planes
OWNER: Jim Roseborough
SIZE: Small (8,000 titles)
SPECIAL SERVICES: Mail orders, special orders
SPECIAL EVENTS: Author signings
GETTING THERE: Rosedale subway station on Yonge line or Bay station on Bloor line; parking on street

The sign on the door reads "DRB Motors, Inc. (Book Division)" and therein lies a tale. DRB Motors began as a restoration shop, with premises located across the street from the present store. The proprietors built a small collection of books to help customers bide their time while waiting for their cars. The restoration business dwindled, the book collection grew, and now DRB Motors survives purely as a bookstore, with titles in air-racing and aerobatics, aviation, biking, car racing (stock, rally, Indy, endurance, and drag), children, coach-building, general military, helicopters, motorcycles, off-road dirt bikes, racing, radio-controlled boats, railroading, railways, restoration, technical manuals, trucks, and off-road vehicles. There are books devoted to particular car-makers, such as Allard, Ferrari, Jaguar, Jensen, Corvette, Lancia, Mercedes-Benz, Morgan, Porsch, Renault, Rover, and Toyota, and airplane manufacturers, such as Beech, Boeing, Sopwith, Vickers, etc. The store also carries calendars featuring automobiles and a dozen British automobile magazines.

DAVID MASON BOOKS

342 Queen Street West, 2nd Floor
(east of Spadina Avenue)
Toronto, Ontario M5V 2A2
416-598-1015 (FAX 416-598-3994)

SPECIALTY: Fine and rare books
OWNER: David Mason
SIZE: Large (50,000 volumes)
SPECIAL SERVICES: Issues catalogues, maintains card-file for individuals in certain subject areas
SPECIAL EVENTS: N/A
GETTING THERE: Osgoode subway station; metered parking on street

The days of the large, general rare bookstore appear to be numbered, as the requisite large floor space conflicts with the realities of downtown real estate prices. Instead, dealers in rare books tend to specialize in particular areas — in the case of David Mason, first editions in literature, women, and travel. The second-storey bookstore, with wooden floors, glassed cases and ceiling fans, fits one's image of what an antiquarian bookstore should look like, and the detailed knowledge of the staff reflects years of meticulous training in the craft and tradition of fine books. The catalogues, published five or six times a year in different areas, contain detailed information required by specialist collectors. This is truly one of the city's finest antiquarian bookstores.

DAVID MIRVISH BOOKS AND BOOKS ON ART

595 Markham Street
(south of Bloor)
Toronto, Ontario M6G 2L8
416-531-9975 (FAX 416-531-5543)

SPECIALTY: Visual arts, photography, architecture, art history
OWNER: David Mirvish
SIZE: Medium (30,000 titles)
SPECIAL SERVICES: Mail orders, special orders
SPECIAL EVENTS: Occasional autographing and exhibitions
GETTING THERE: Markham Street exit from Bathurst subway station; parking on street

The area around Bloor and Bathurst which contains Mirvish Village has become one of the more colourful and charming parts of the city, with antique lampposts, open-air terraces, stained-glass windows, quirkily painted buildings, coffee houses, art galleries, and handmade crafts. During our visit, a knife-sharpener walked by, ringing his bell. In the heart of Mirvish Village lies David Mirvish Books, which merits a visit if only to see the enormous Frank Stella painting (*Damascus Gate Stretch Variation* I [1970]) whose joyful interweaving of coloured arcs serves as the main backdrop to a large, airy display space. The collection includes biography, Canadian art history, children's books, crafts, decorative arts, essays and ideas, fiction, history of design, Judaica, Latin American art, native arts, painting techniques, photography, typography, and women's issues. Tables of remaindered items include real bargains on "coffee-table" art books. The high ceilings permit a display of artwork on the walls above the bookshelves which, along with soft classical music in the background, makes the store a pleasure for browsing.

DENCAN BOOKS AND STAMPS

3113 Dundas Street West
(between Keele and Runnymede)
Toronto, Ontario M6P 1Z9
416-763-2302 (No FAX)

SPECIALTY: Stamps, coins, pocketbooks, magazines
OWNER: Harold Peterson
SIZE: Small
SPECIAL SERVICES: Layaway plans
SPECIAL EVENTS: N/A
GETTING THERE: Dundas subway station on Bloor line and Junction bus or High Park or Runnymede; parking on street

Dencan Books and Stamps buys, sells, and trades books. The books for sale comprise mostly used pocketbooks stacked several deep on the shelves in the most popular categories for casual readers: fiction, horror, mystery, romance, true crime, war, westerns. There are several bins of comics, and bunches of hardcover books selling for 50¢.

DRAGON LADY COMIC SHOP

200 Queen Street West
(near University)
Toronto, Ontario M5V 1Z2
416-596-1602 (No fax)

SPECIALTY: Comic books, mainstream comics, *Star Trek* memorabilia, current and used
OWNER: John Burnett
SIZE: Medium (10,000 titles)
SPECIAL SERVICES: N/A
SPECIAL EVENTS: N/A
GETTING THERE: Queen Street streetcar; metered parking on street

Comic books are generally issued once a month. Dragon Lady carries current copies of mainstream comics such as *Batman, Superman, Swamp Thing, The Mighty Thor, Vampirella*, and *Star Trek*, as well as a number of mini-comics sold on consignment. The number of different comic books published staggers the imagination. In the S's alone, one finds *Spirit of Vengeance, Sandman, Scarlet Letter, Silver Surfer, Spawn, Solitaire, Spectre, Steel, Savage Drag*, and *The Shroud*. Searching for back issues in a confined space can be a chore, but the low prices justify the effort. Dragon Lady's second location in Mirvish Village (600 Markham Street, 2nd Floor, 416-536-7460) has space to include old advertising, vintage magazines (1900–1980) including birthday *Life* issues, movie and sports memorabilia, children's illustrated books, and original artwork.

DUKA LA HARAMBEE

71 McCaul Street
(between Dundas and Queen)
Toronto, Ontario M5T 2W7
416-593-7650 (FAX 416-599-0759)

SPECIALTY: Multicultural, African-focus material
OWNER: Harambee Foundation
SIZE: Small
SPECIAL SERVICES: Educational guidance, workshops, seminars
SPECIAL EVENTS: Literary fair, readings, Kwanzaa festival
GETTING THERE: Dundas or Queen Street streetcars, Osgoode or St. Patrick subway station; parking on street

Duka la Harambee offers a variety of titles in three categories: children's books (high interest, low vocabulary books for early readers); history; light literature. The store specializes in educational materials and offers to evaluate textbooks for teachers and advise on their use across the curriculum. Here, teachers can obtain books on India, Guatemala, Kenya, and other Third World countries. The store holds an annual Kwanzaa festival, an event comparable in African cultures to Christmas, essentially a celebration of family and community values. The store features reading and enrichment materials focusing on the family.

DUNHUANG BOOKS AND ARTS

328 Broadview Avenue
(between Dundas and Gerrard)
Toronto, Ontario M4M 2Z9
416-465-8266 (FAX same)

SPECIALTY: Chinese books
OWNER: Mai Chu
SIZE: Small
SPECIAL SERVICES: N/A
SPECIAL EVENTS: N/A
GETTING THERE: Broadview subway station on Bloor line; parking on street

Dunhuang Books and Arts offers titles in Chinese in a great variety of fields: art, calligraphy, children's books, classical literature, computer books (quite old), contemporary literature, cooking, entertainment and sports, fashion and hairstyle, fitness, gardening, history and geography, martial arts, medicine, music and arts (including Peking opera), novels and short stories, science fiction, self-improvement, sociology, technical books on automobiles and design, textbooks old and new. There are also English translations of Chinese literature and books in English on Chinese politics, history, and economics. In addition to the usual English/Chinese and Vietnamese/Chinese dictionaries, the store carries technical dictionaries on geography, electronics, and medicine.

ED'S BOOKS

2442 Danforth Avenue
(near Main Street)
Toronto, Ontario M4C 1K9
416-691-3187 (No FAX)

SPECIALTY: Used books, all kinds
OWNER: Hendra Tanuwidjaja
SIZE: Small
SPECIAL SERVICES: N/A
SPECIAL EVENTS: N/A
GETTING THERE: Main subway station on the Bloor line; parking on street

Ed's Books is the only bookstore in the city that also sells ice cream! The store buys, sells, and trades paperback books, mostly light reading, displayed on metal racks facing forward, with four or five books to the stack, so you really have to hunt. Categories include adventure, cookbooks, fantasy, general fiction, Harlequin novels, mystery, romance (by far the largest section), and westerns. The new owner, Hendra Tanuwidjaja, reports that the business has grown rapidly to include both retail and wholesale business. The store now carries records, CDs, and cassettes in addition to books. This neighbourhood store is open only in the afternoons.

ED'S USED BOOKS

957 Kingston Road
(near Scarborough Road)
Toronto, Ontario M4E 1S8
No telephone or fax

SPECIALTY: Used books bought, sold, and traded
OWNER: Ed
SIZE: Very small
SPECIAL SERVICES: N/A
SPECIAL EVENTS: N/A
GETTING THERE: Kingston streetcar; parking on street

Ed's Used Books, like most neighbourhood used book-stores, sells primarily mass market paperbacks: romances, science fiction, biography, mystery, and adventure. Many books are stacked five or six deep in metal bins so that you have no way of knowing what lies behind the top layer. Ed's regular customers display a loyal affinity to the owner, seeking his advice for weekend reading material. The front window displays hundreds of books set on edge for the benefit of side-walk browsers, while the walls are covered with framed pictures of Bing Crosby, Elvis, and other celebrities.

EDWARDS BOOKS & ART

356 Queen Street West
(Main Office)
Toronto, Ontario M5V 2A2
416-593-0126 (FAX 416-596-1528)

SPECIALTY: General books with an emphasis on art
OWNER: Edward and Eva Borins
SIZE: Medium
SPECIAL SERVICES: Special orders, mail orders, out-of-print searches
SPECIAL EVENTS: Author signings and book launches

The Edwards bookstores seem to have been designed to appeal to browsers. There are long, flat tables with books piled face up. The multitude of covers seizes the eye and the imagination. There are many tables of remainder books and discounted books, the entire central section of the store in some locations, and many trade paperbacks for the discerning but budget-conscious book collector. One finds books on architecture, art, children's literature, cooking, crafts, fiction, health, humour, performing arts, reference, science and nature, and travel. The Queen West store and Park Plaza store (170 Bloor West at Avenue Road) have numerous out-of-print and rare books in stock. There are currently five stores in the Metro area: 356 Queen Street West (416-593-0126); 170 Bloor Street West (416-961-2428); 2200 Yonge Street (416-487-5431); 2179 Queen Street East (698-1442); 8147 Yonge Street, Thornhill (905-731-3050).

ELIOT'S BOOKSHOP

584 Yonge Street
(north of Wellesley)
Toronto, Ontario M4Y 1Z3
416-925-0258 (No FAX)

SPECIALTY: General used books on three floors
OWNER: Paul Panayiotidis
SIZE: Large
SPECIAL SERVICES: N/A
SPECIAL EVENTS: N/A
GETTING THERE: Wellesley subway station; parking on side streets

Eliot's Bookshop takes one by surprise: how can such a large used bookstore exist right in the centre of the city? For this is a used bookstore in the classic tradition, containing all the books you used to own yourself but sold or gave away over the years, plus all the books you remember seeing on library shelves. The first floor has thirty categories of books ranging (alphabetically) from Adventures/Westerns to True Crime; the second floor, nine categories from Amerindian and Native Issues to War; and the third floor, eighteen categories from Acting to Women's Studies. There are ten shelves on classical music on the third floor and shelf after shelf of mysteries. Under plays, I found seven copies of T.S. Eliot's *The Cocktail Party*, fourteen of *Murder in the Cathedral*, and seven of *The Family Reunion*. The first floor, with bookcases stretching ten shelves high to the ceiling, contains mostly paperbacks, with hardbound books primarily on the upper floors. A "new arrivals" section permits regular customers to inspect incoming books before they disappear into the vastness of the general collection.

EMERALD COMICS AND SPORTSCARDS

1431 Kingston Road
(near Warden Avenue)
Scarborough, Ontario M1N 1R4
416-694-3211 (FAX same)

SPECIALTY: Old and new comics and sports cards, collectibles, posters
OWNER: Steve Kalaitzidis
SIZE: Small
SPECIAL SERVICES: Subscription service, laminating service, fax service
SPECIAL EVENTS: N/A
GETTING THERE: Warden subway station and Kingston Road bus; parking on street

Emerald Comics is a single-room neighbourhood store offering primarily mainline comics from the Silver Age (1956–1970) to the present. Marvel and Image comics, the primary publishers represented in the store, occupy separate alphabetical files. Other bins contain a number of independent publishers including Tops, Dark Horse and Harris. Owner Steve Kalaitzidis notes that the main problem of comic book stores is inventory control. He is in the process of acquiring warehouse space to assure an orderly arrangement of his inventory.

EVANS — THE BUSINESS BOOK STORE

11 Irwin Avenue
(off Yonge Street)
Toronto, Ontario M4Y 1L1
416-964-0161 (FAX 416-964-7305)

SPECIALTY: Accounting, auditing, taxation and finance, student materials
OWNER: Paul Evans
SIZE: Small
SPECIAL SERVICES: Textbooks, special orders, mail orders
SPECIAL EVENTS: N/A
GETTING THERE: Wellesley subway station; parking on street

Evans — The Business Book Store, serves primarily as the campus bookstore for the International Academy, the Canadian School of Management, Wordsworth College, and for students in chartered accounting at University of Toronto and elsewhere. It also serves the business community with books on accounting, business law, economics, finance, management control systems, management and administration, marketing, personal finance, and taxation. In addition, the store supplies books for the Society of Actuaries. The owner is currently preparing a catalogue.

EXCALIBUR COMICS

3030 Bloor Street West
(near Royal York)
Toronto, Ontario M8X 1C4
416-236-3553 (NO FAX)

SPECIALTY: Comic books, new and collectibles
OWNER: Robert Chin
SIZE: Small
SPECIAL SERVICES: Want lists
SPECIAL EVENTS: N/A
GETTING THERE: Royal York subway station; metered parking on street

Excalibur Comics is a tiny store, 15 ft. x 15 ft., but still has lots of comics, arranged in bins, which you can inspect practically by turning a complete circle. Though there is room for only five or six customers at a time (depending on how slim they are), the bins contain quite a number of comics, which are also displayed all over the walls.

FEDERAL PUBLICATIONS, INC.

165 University Avenue
(near Adelaide)
Toronto, Ontario M5H 3B8
416-860-1611 (FAX 416-860-1608)

SPECIALTY: Federal government publications, OECD publications, maps, charts
OWNER: Denis Atha
SIZE: Small
SPECIAL SERVICES: Business by mail, special orders
SPECIAL EVENTS: N/A
GETTING THERE: St. Andrew subway station on University line; parking in muncipal lots

Governments are the largest publishers in the world. Federal Publications, Inc., known as "The Government Book Store," attracts a diverse clientele of business people, lawyers, immigration consultants, hospital nutritionists, hikers, canoers, and campers since it offers materials in a wide variety of areas including aboriginal issues, agriculture, economics, education, energy, environment, history, immigration, language, natural resources, taxation, technology, and transport. In addition to Canadian government publications, the store carries selected international government publications. (The store does not carry provincial or municipal government publications.)

GARDEN ROOM BOOKS

921 Queen Street West
(4 blocks west of Bathurst)
Toronto, Ontario M6J 1G5
416-504-1417 (No FAX)

SPECIALTY: New and used gardening books
OWNER: Michaela Keenan
SIZE: Very small
SPECIAL SERVICES: Searches, mail orders
SPECIAL EVENTS: Workshops, seminars, small tours
GETTING THERE: Queen Street streetcar or Ossington bus from Ossington subway station; parking on street

A gardening bookstore in the middle of a large city offers, as one might expect, a number of books on gardening in the city, such as container gardening and raising plants on small plots of land. Being a Canadian bookstore, it carries a fair number of books with titles like *Cold Climate Gardening*. In addition to ordinary gardening books, this store sells a fine selection of literary garden books by "gardener writers" including Katherine S. White's *Onward and Upward in the Garden* and Eleanor Perényi's much requested *Green Thoughts: A Writer in the Garden*, as well as books on the history of garden design and biographies of designers.

GIFTS FROM THE EARTH

320 Danforth Avenue
(near Broadview)
Toronto, Ontario M4K 1N8
416-465-4579 (No FAX)

SPECIALTY: Rocks and minerals, books on rocks and minerals, New Age books
OWNER: Ashtanga Yoga Fellowship
SIZE: Small
SPECIAL SERVICES: N/A
SPECIAL EVENTS: N/A
GETTING THERE: Chester subway station on Bloor line; parking on street and parking lot behind store located in Carrot Common

Gifts from the Earth sells all manner of crystals and minerals, each labelled according to its metaphysical properties (e.g., "Agate — stabilizes, cleansing effect; good for stimulating analytical capabilities and precision; strengthens sight"). The book collection, currently being expanded, includes books on yoga, meditation, metaphysical properties of minerals, aromatherapy, astrology, ashtanga yoga, crystal healing and divination, and herbal remedies. A typical title is *The Crystal Book: Explore the Amazing World of the Quartz Crystal and Its Use as a Tool for Harnessing Mind Energy*. The store also sells meditation cassettes and CDs.

GLAD DAY BOOKSHOP

598A Yonge Street, 2nd floor
(north of Wellesley)
Toronto, Ontario M4Y 1Z3
416-961-4161 (FAX 416-961-1624)

SPECIALTY: Gay and lesbian literature
OWNER: John Scythes
SIZE: Medium (11,000 books)
SPECIAL SERVICES: Mail orders, special orders, monthly newsletter of new titles
SPECIAL EVENTS: Readings with authors, tables for Gay Pride Day
GETTING THERE: Wellesley subway station; metered parking on side streets

Glad Day Bookshop symbolizes the intersection of literature and politics, not only in the nature of its collection but in its continuing dispute with the Canadian customs office over the importation of books and magazines into the store. The store appears to be thriving, for all this, and serves as a focus for the city's gay community, with books in English, French, Spanish, and Italian on AIDS (subdivided into children's literature, biological aspects, and self-help), alcoholism and addiction, Asian literature, astrology, bisexuality, Black identity, cinema studies, coming out, feminism, freedom of speech, gay/lesbian topics from autobiography to travel guides, goddess studies, literary criticism, male identity, native identity, political activism, religion, science fiction and fantasy, sexual abuse, transsexuality, and transvestism. In addition, one finds many sections on individual people, including W.H. Auden, Quentin Crisp, Allen Ginsberg, Yves Navare, and Oscar Wilde. The store also carries a large stock of journals and magazines.

GREEN GABLES BOOKS

118 Main Street North
(Highway 48 off Route 7)
Markham, Ontario L3P 1Y1
905-294-4773 (FAX 905-294-0065)

SPECIALTY: General, education
OWNER: David Levin
SIZE: Medium
SPECIAL SERVICES: Special orders, mail orders, particularly in children's education, wellness, Attention Deficit Disorder, and parenting
SPECIAL EVENTS: Enrichment classes in reading, poetry, and adult education
GETTING THERE: Main Markham bus up Main Street; parking on street

Green Gables Books specializes in reading: during the winter, ninety kids a week are registered in pre-school reading programs; in the evening, high school students come in for courses in poetry, the novel, and creative writing. These enrichment programs serve both to promote reading and writing skills and to attract people to the bookstore, which sells literature for children and adults, as well as books on business, cooking, gardening, parenting, travel, and wellness. The store issues a newsletter six times a year with recommendations by owner, staff, and customers. The store also sponsors a BookMobile which travels to schools, hospitals, and other health care institutions with a stock of books geared to people in those locations.

GREY REGION

226 Queen Street West
(between John and McCaul)
Toronto, Ontario M5V 1Z6
416-974-9211 (No FAX)

SPECIALTY: Comic books
OWNER: Michael Teodori and Phillip Teodori
SIZE: Medium
SPECIAL SERVICES: Reserves, 10% discount for members
SPECIAL EVENTS: End-of-month sales offer 50% off back issues
GETTING THERE: Osgoode subway station on University line; metered parking on street

Comic-book stores in the city, like bookstores, may be separated into neighbourhood stores, where one can obtain current, popular books, and stores such as Grey Region where one comes to look for particular items. Under "S" one may find *Sleepwalker, Silver Surfer, Silver Sabre, She Hulk, Savage She Hulk, Show Case, Span, Solo Avengers, Solar Man of the Atom, Spectre, Squadron Supreme, Spitfire, Storm Watch, Suicide Squad, Superboy, Supergirl,* and *Submariner*. In addition to comics published by the three mainstream firms, DC, Valiant, and Marvel, the store carries role-playing games, new and used fantasy miniatures, posters and T-shirts, baseball and sports cards.

HAIRY TARANTULA COMICS AND CARDS LTD.

354½A Yonge Street
Toronto, Ontario M5B 1S5
416-596-8002 (No FAX)

SPECIALTY: Alternative comics and games
OWNER: Leon Emmett
SIZE: Large
SPECIAL SERVICES: Membership card (services include discounts and reserves); assistance with games
SPECIAL EVENTS: Demonstrations of games
GETTING THERE: Dundas subway station; near World's Biggest Bookstore

The Hairy Tarantula merits a visit if only for a view of its unforgettably oversize eponymous mascot. The collection includes lots of old, rare and Silver Age books (ca. 1956–1970), as well as a nearly complete run of mainstream comics from 1962 to 1980. The store carries many independent comics not found elsewhere (small press, alternative, or Japanese comics). Here you will also find movie-related comics, reprints of comics from the 1950s, underground comics from the 1960s, all the Disney and Archie comics. Under "S" I found *Savage Dragon, Scarlett, Sebastian O, Secret Defenders, Secret Weapons, Shape-Changing Man, Shadowmasks, Shadowhaunt, Showcase, Solar, Spectacular Spider,* and *Suicide Squad.* The store manages to carry an enormous number of comics in a small space, with more in storage.

HALF PRICE BOOKS AND MUSIC

1560 Bayview Avenue (near Davisville)
Toronto, Ontario M4G 3B8
416-440-4253 (No FAX)

SPECIALTY: General used books and CDs
OWNER: Steve Gosewich
SIZE: Medium (2,700 square feet at Bayview; 4,000 square feet in the Beaches)
SPECIAL SERVICES: Customer requests; listen to CDs before buying them; 10% seniors discount; 10% teacher/library discount; frequent reader card
SPECIAL EVENTS: N/A
GETTING THERE: Davisville subway station, #11 Bayview bus; parking on street

Half Price Books and Music is a great place to find reading at a bargain. Spacious, well-lighted, attractive shelves arranged in a series of alcoves offer mystery and spy thriller (fourteen bookcases, floor to ceiling), science fiction, horror, romance, Harlequin novels, history, and children's books, with smaller sections devoted to fiction, humour, television, film, music, poetry. The title of the store underestimates the savings it offers: I found hardbound copies of Pierre Berton, *The Last Spike* at $1.99, John Updike, *The Coup* at $2.99, and John Barth, *Letters* at $2.99. Romances sell at two for 99¢. There is a second store in the Beaches at 1939 Queen Street East (telephone 416-699-5511).

HANDY BOOK EXCHANGE

1762 Avenue Road
(near Melrose Avenue)
Toronto, Ontario M5M 3Y9
416-781-4139 (No FAX)

SPECIALTY: New and used books
OWNER: Olive Navis
SIZE: Large
SPECIAL SERVICES: Owner chooses books for regular customers, having come to know their tastes
SPECIAL EVENTS: Occasional author signings
GETTING THERE: Bus from Yonge and Eglinton; parking on street

The Handy Book Exchange has been aptly described in *Discovery Magazine* as "one of the tidiest and best organized of Toronto's used bookstores." Never have mass-market paperbacks been displayed with such loving care. The books are arranged in alcoves of labelled bookcases, specially designed to fit exactly this format of book. Not only are the books alphabetized by author, but individual shelves are designated by letter. This said, it remains a neighbourhood bookstore composed primarily of general fiction (with a tendency toward "bodice-rippers"), with particular strengths in mysteries (eighteen bookcases) and children's books (an entire alcove). The latest bestsellers are available for rental in hardcover form; otherwise, the books are all paperbacks.

HOLLYWOOD CANTEEN

1516 Danforth Avenue
(west of Coxwell)
Toronto, Ontario M4J 1N4
416-461-1704 (No FAX)

SPECIALTY: Original movie memorabilia, classic video rentals and sales, cinema books, new and used
OWNER: Michael Orlando
SIZE: Medium
SPECIAL SERVICES: Book searches
SPECIAL EVENTS: In-store autographing
GETTING THERE: Coxwell subway station on Bloor line; parking on street

Hollywood Canteen is a delight for movie buffs, with movie posters covering the walls, models of famous stars decking the bookcases, and 8" x 10" stills filling several file cabinets. The store rents or sells videos of classic films as well as posters and postcards. The book collection itself covers every aspect of moviemaking, including autobiography/biography, comedy, directors, *film noir*, film history, theory and criticism, foreign filmmaking, musicals, screenplays, script-writing, scripts, special effects, studio books, technical guides to film and video, television, westerns, and writers. Scholars of the cinema will find academic books from university presses; fans of Marilyn Monroe will find an entire bookcase devoted to the star. The store maintains a large collection of out-of-print books and has many more items in storage, constituting North America's largest inventory of film books, past and present.

ISLAMIC BOOK SERVICE

1272B The Queensway
(beside Kipling)
Etobicoke, Ontario M8Z 1R5
416-416-503-9197 (FAX same)

SPECIALTY: Islamic books
OWNER: Islamic Society of North America; Ali Baksh, manager
SIZE: Small (400 titles)
SPECIAL SERVICES: N/A
SPECIAL EVENTS: N/A
GETTING THERE: Kipling subway station; parking in front or back of store

Islamic Book Service serves as a mail-order and walk-in centre for the network maintained by the Islamic Society of North America. The store, decorated with hanging rugs, posters, and pictures, displays its books face out on shelves. A large section is devoted to editions of, general studies of, and interpretations of the Holy Qur'an. The manager explains that the Islamic Society is devoted to the truth, so one will find books on Arabic, biographies of the prophet Muhammad, biography, calligraphy, children's books, comparative religion, dictionaries, economics, education, family, history, Islam and politics, Islam and the family, Islam and education, Islam and the West, Islamic art, law, philosophy, politics, reference, religion, science, science and interpretation of Hadith, and society, but no fiction, for fiction is not the truth.

ISLAMIC BOOKS AND SOUVENIRS

1395 Gerrard Street East
(near Greenwood)
Toronto, Ontario M4L 1Z3
416-778-8461 (FAX 416-462-1832)

SPECIALTY: Books and souvenirs on Islam
OWNER: Shamim Ahmad
SIZE: Small
SPECIAL SERVICES: N/A
SPECIAL EVENTS: N/A
GETTING THERE: Gerrard streetcar; parking on street

Islamic Books and Souvenirs carries books on a variety of subjects centering on the Muslim faith, such as *Muslim Parents: Their Rights and Duties*, *Islam Forbids Free Mixing of Men and Women*, *The Myth of the Cross*, and *1,000 Questions on Islam*. The store offers beautifully bound copies of the Qur'an, commentaries thereupon, translations in fifteen languages, books on death, Muhammad, Salat (prayer books), Urdu (a language of India and Pakistan), books on general topics such as *Islamic Jurisprudence in the Modern World*, children's books, prayer rugs and beads, and other aids to religious practice. Tapes, CDs, videos and plaques are also available.

ISRAEL'S THE JUDAICA CENTRE

897 Eglinton Avenue West
(near Bathurst)
Toronto, Ontario M6C 2CI
416-256-1010 (FAX 416-256-2750)

SPECIALTY: Hebrew texts, religious items, children's Judaica, giftware, records and cassettes
OWNER: Israel Kaplan
SIZE: Medium (25,000 volumes)
SPECIAL SERVICES: Gift-wrapping, delivery, mail orders, wedding and bar mitzvah service within the Jewish community
SPECIAL EVENTS: Occasional author signings
GETTING THERE: Bus from Eglinton West subway station; parking nearby

A strong sense of family and community creates an exceptionally warm, welcoming atmosphere at Israel's. High on the walls are beautiful framed *Ketuba* — artistic certificates for weddings — as the friendly clerk explained to me. The collection includes cookbooks, fiction, Hebrew dictionaries, books on the Bible, holidays, the Holocaust, humour and trivia, Israel, Jewish holidays, Jewish thought, prayer and prayerbooks, as well as children's books on all the holidays, the Bible, the Holocaust, and literature. A second outlet is located in Thornhill at 441 Clark Avenue, north of Steeles between Bathurst and Yonge (905-881-1010, FAX 905-881-1016).

ITALBOOK — LIBRERIA ITALIANA

1337 St. Clair Avenue West
(near Lansdowne)
Toronto, Ontario M6E IC3
416-651-3310 (FAX 416-654-5957)

SPECIALTY: General bookstore containing books printed in Italy
OWNER: Mario Giacobbi
SIZE: Small (2,000 books)
SPECIAL SERVICES: Delivery
SPECIAL EVENTS: N/A
GETTING THERE: St. Clair streetcar; parking on street

Italbook is a neighbourhood bookstore serving an area which has been, until recently, strongly Italian. The attractive window display is filled with books, flags, globes, and stuffed animals. At the same time, Italbook supplies titles for local universities since it orders books directly from Italian publishers rather than going through an intermediary. The shelves contain paperbacks, novels with uncut pages, and scholarly editions, side by side. The wooden bookcases contain works in Italian on art, cooking, gardening, health, history (especially of Greece, Rome, and Italy), maps, religion, travel, women's issues, as well as English translations of Italian literature and Italian translations of American best-sellers. One will also find a large selection of children's books. Prices tend to be high because of the small print runs by Italian publishers. (Ten thousand would be considered a large edition.) Visiting the bookstore brings one to an attractive neighbourhood where street signs still read Via Dufferino (for Dufferin Street) and Via Italia (for St. Clair Avenue).

JAMIE FRASER BOOKS

479A Queen Street West
(near Spadina)
Toronto, Ontario M5V 2A9
416-504-2391 (NO FAX)

SPECIALTY: Mystery, science fiction and fantasy, pulp fiction

OWNER: Jamie Fraser

SIZE: Small (3,000 paperbacks, 6,000 hardcover books)

SPECIAL SERVICES: Book searches, minor repair and cleaning of books, appraisals (from ten books to entire estates)

SPECIAL EVENTS: Author signings, bookseller parties

GETTING THERE: Queen Street streetcar, Spadina subway and Spadina bus; five-minute walk from Osgood Subway; parking lots nearby

Jamie Fraser Books is a serious bookstore devoted to genre fiction. The small stock specializes in modern first editions, detective fiction, science fiction, fantasy, rare paperback originals and pulp magazines along the lines of *The Shadow*, *Weird Tales*, *Amazing Stories*, and *Black Mask*. A copy of Rex Stout's *Death of a Doxy*, which sold for $3.75 in 1966, now sells for $45. Do not confuse this bookstore with neighbourhood stores that sell popular editions of mysteries and science fiction. Owner Jamie Fraser caters as much to book collectors as to book readers, and has brought considerable experience as a book dealer to building this collection. The second-floor shop is located across the hall from Robert Wright Books.

JOHN LORD'S BOOKS

6356 Main Street
(near Highway 48)
Stouffville, Ontario L4A 7Z7
905-640-3579 (FAX 905-640-4488)

SPECIALTY: Used and new books

OWNER: John Lord

SIZE: Large (warehouse has 25,000 used books; store has 45,000 used and 20,000 new)

SPECIAL SERVICES: Special orders, general searches

SPECIAL EVENTS: Half-price used book sales in February and September; occasional autographings

GETTING THERE: Forty-five minutes from downtown Toronto. North on Don Valley Parkway and 404, exit at Stouffville Road, and go east for 10 minutes. The store is located in the centre of the town. Parking on street.

John Lord's Books carries new and used books in art, biography, Canadiana, exploration, fiction, history, military history, natural history, the occult, poetry, railways, travel, equestrianism, and New Zealand. The collection includes a large selection of children's books. Individual sections are often as strong as those of smaller specialty stores in Toronto. The store periodically issues catalogues.

JOSEPHS INSPIRATIONAL SERVICES, INC.

2721 Markham Road, Unit 39
(north of Finch)
Toronto, Ontario M1X 1L5
416-291-1772 (FAX 416-291-1378)

SPECIALTY: Inspirational books, mainly Catholic; church supplies, chalices, gifts, clergy shirts
OWNER: Joseph Rizza
SIZE: Small
SPECIAL SERVICES: Special order
SPECIAL EVENTS: N/A
GETTING THERE: Scarborough Town Centre LRT station; free parking

Josephs Inspirational Services provides primary material for teachers, with all kinds of practical books on issues that teachers face, such as children and divorce. Children's books include prayers, Bible atlases, and the Catholic Children's Bible. There are books for youth such as *Creative Conflict Solving for Kids* and *Morality and Youth: Fostering Christian Identity*. The store also offers books on Christian living, parenting, mental health, prayers, teaching tools, and women's issues, primarily from a Roman Catholic orientation.

KEW BEACH GALLERIES

2008 Queen Street East
(near Bellfair Avenue)
Toronto, Ontario M4L 1J3
416-694-5915 (No FAX)

SPECIALTY: Used books
OWNER: Unidentified
SIZE: Very small
SPECIAL SERVICES: N/A
SPECIAL EVENTS: N/A
GETTING THERE: Queen Street streetcar; parking on street

Kew Beach Galleries represents a used bookstore of a bygone generation, with dated books on miscellaneous subjects, as well as ancient best-sellers, a bit of bric-à-brac, and some antiques.

KIDS ARE WORTH IT, BY MOYER'S

Yorkdale Shopping Centre
3401 Dufferin Street, Suite 1019
Toronto, Ontario M6A 2T9
416-256-7206 (FAX 416-729-7846)

SPECIALTY: Children's educational materials
OWNER: Moyer's Learning World Group
SIZE: Small
SPECIAL SERVICES: Special orders, holds, phone-in orders
SPECIAL EVENTS: Occasional special appearances for autographing
GETTING THERE: Yorkdale subway station; parking in Yorkdale Mall

Take the children to Kids Are Worth It and watch them enjoy the fountains, light-show display, stuffed animals, and a small "theatre" showing Barney videos. Giant signs indicate each category (a large software section is labelled "Future"). There are lots of nooks, almost small arcades. The store issues a 460-page catalogue which includes 41 pages of children's books and 27 pages of art and craft books and materials, with other books on geography, language arts, mathematics, and science. Kids Are Worth It contains everything a teacher could want to delight a classroom of children, or a parent, to occupy a child on a rainy afternoon. (See also the entry under Moyer's, Kids Are Worth It.)

KIDS AT PLAY

2184C Bloor Street West
(near Runnymede)
Toronto, Ontario M6S 1N3
416-766-4731 (FAX 416-766-8470)

SPECIALTY: Children's books, especially arts and crafts
OWNER: The Toy Shop (62 Cumberland Street)
SIZE: Small
SPECIAL SERVICES: Special orders
SPECIAL EVENTS: Free activities during March break — workshops in lobby of theatre below
GETTING THERE: Runnymede subway station on Bloor line; public parking behind store

While primarily a toy store, Kids at Play has an interesting section of children's books, arranged thematically. The nature area includes a number of "Eyewitness Books," beautifully photographed, containing lots of information. In the travel section one can find books on activities for the road, activities for the cottage, a treasury of games, and touring books such as *Places to Go, People to See, Things to Do — All Across Canada*. The "School Zone" display contains pedagogical books such as spelling puzzles, rhyming pictures, phonics review, fractions, and mazes. A section of children's literature contains the classics as well as boxed sets such as the Baby-Sitters Club and Nancy Drew. Other categories include arts, chapter books, cookbooks, fairy tales, oversize books, picture books, poetry, and pop-up books. Parents may wish to take note of the March break activities: one year, the author of *Bridges* helped kids build bridges; another time, an author of a book on codes and riddles worked on codes with children.

THE LANGUAGE CENTRE BOOKSTORE

1100 Eglinton Avenue West
(near Allen Road)
Toronto, Ontario M6C 2E2
416-787-4507 (FAX 416-781-5508)

SPECIALTY: Books on
English-as-a-Second-Language (ESL)
OWNER: Stephanie Paulauskas and Susanne
Holunga
SIZE: Small
SPECIAL SERVICES: Consulting with universities,
special contracts to develop ESL programs
SPECIAL EVENTS: Private or small-group tutoring
in store, teacher training courses
GETTING THERE: Eglinton West subway station;
parking on side streets

According to the United Nations, Toronto is among the most culturally diverse cities in the world, with some 130 identifiable ethnic groups. Small wonder that local schools and universities offer an abundance of ESL programs. The Language Centre Bookstore specializes in supplying materials for these programs. For children, there are classic stories, graded readers, and basic books for children age three and up just starting to read. For adult immigrants, there are materials directed to beginners as well as advanced learners. The owners, both of whom hold doctorates in ESL, offer expert guidance in selecting classroom materials either for use locally or for those travelling overseas to teach English-as-a-second-language. The store carries some taped materials and videocassettes and is currently expanding into CD-ROMs. The Language Centre Bookstore also provides books, dictionaries, and audiocassettes in other languages such as French, Spanish, Italian, German, etc., for those wishing to learn a foreign language.

LARRY BECKER'S COLLECTIBLES WAREHOUSE

45 Brisbane Road, Unit 6
(west of Dufferin, north of Finch)
Mailing address: Box 1011, Station B
North York, Ontario M2K 2T6
416-661-3175 (FAX 416-740-9890)

SPECIALTY: Military history, corps histories,
Canadiana, transportation (cars, trains, aircraft,
ships), postcards, car dealer brochures, and
international vintage licence plates
OWNER: Larry Becker
SIZE: Medium
SPECIAL SERVICES: Helping collectors find things
they're looking for
SPECIAL EVENTS: N/A
GETTING THERE: Alness Street bus from Wilson
subway station or Finch bus, get off at Dufferin
and walk one block north on Alness; parking at
store

Larry Becker collects things — war medals, badges, uniforms and other militaria, postcards, car brochures, a large collection of coins, licence plates, military medals, international badges and insignia, bound volumes of newspapers, magazines from 1900 to the 1980s, all sorted by year, model cars, postcards, sports cards, stamps, Hollywoodiana — and for thirty years has been displaying them in a warehouse that must be seen to be believed. He also collects books: military books, religious books, books about celebrities, children's books and books on collecting, as well as a small collection of used books on many subjects. This is a fun place to visit; if it doesn't have what you want, it will have dozens of other things you never even imagined.

LATVIAN BOOK STORE

4 Credit Union Drive
(off Eglinton, east of the
Ontario Science Centre)
Toronto, Ontario M4A 2N8
416-757-1482 (No FAX)

SPECIALTY: Books on Latvia and mostly in Latvian language
OWNER: Latvian Relief Society of Canada
SIZE: Small
SPECIAL SERVICES: Mail orders
SPECIAL EVENTS: Events at the Latvian Cultural Centre
GETTING THERE: Bus #34 from Eglinton subway station; parking at building

The Latvian Book Store occupies one room of the sizeable Latvian Canadian Cultural Centre, which also sponsors classes, musical activities, lectures, a heritage display and a library. The book collection includes grammars and other materials for learning Latvian, Bibles and religious books, children's books (with Donald Duck, Yogi Bear and The Little Mermaid in Latvian translations), songbooks, Latvian literature, and books on arts and crafts, history, poetry, and politics. The store carries a number of magazines and newspapers published both in Latvia and in Toronto, including *Latvija Amerika*, a weekly published in Toronto, along with arts, crafts and all kinds of gift items.

THE LAW BOOKSTORE

166 Bullock Drive, Unit 8
(near McCowan and Highway 7)
Markham, Ontario L3P 1W2
905-472-0219 (FAX 905-472-5578)
http://www.airlink.org/lawbook/

SPECIALTY: Law and true crime
OWNER: Jack L. Heath
SIZE: Medium (15,000 to 20,000 titles)
SPECIAL SERVICES: Book searches
SPECIAL EVENTS: N/A
GETTING THERE: McCowan bus; free parking in front of store

The Law Bookstore, the only full-time law bookstore in Canada, sells new and used law books to lawyers, law firms and law school libraries throughout the British Commonwealth and around the world. The store buys from estates, law firms and disbarred or bankrupt lawyers. In addition to current books on aviation, corporate, criminal, environmental and patent law, the store sells rare books such as a Canadian Police Manual from 1775 written in Old French, one of about twenty copies produced. One may also find legal biographies, courtroom dramas, and other books on true crime. The store issues regular catalogues of law reports, back runs of law journals, out-of-print and rare books.

LEGENDS OF THE GAME

322A King Street West
(near John)
Toronto, Ontario M5V 1J2
416-971-8848 (FAX 416-971-9360)

SPECIALTY: Comic books, sports memorabilia
OWNER: Wally Boshyk
SIZE: Small
SPECIAL SERVICES: Free subscription service
SPECIAL EVENTS: Occasional sports celebrity signings
GETTING THERE: King Street streetcar; parking lots and meter parking

You know you're in a sports store from the minute you pull the baseball bats that serve as door handles and enter a large room with sports shirts hanging from the ceiling. Comics occupy one section of the store in the usual display format: new issues, last week's comics, and a large number of comics neatly displayed in well-labelled bins. The store sells mostly mainline comics; the "S" section includes *Shaman's Tears*, *Simpson's*, *Solar: Man of the Atom*, *Spiderman 2099*, *Spirits of Vengeance*, *Star Wars — Dark Horse*, *Steel*, *Storm Watch*, *Strange Tales*, and *Supreme*.

LIBRITAL ITALIAN BOOK CENTRE

2908 Dufferin Street
(south of Lawrence)
Toronto, Ontario M6B 3S8
416-789-2181 (FAX 416-789-2182)

SPECIALTY: Academic books in Italian
OWNER: Marti Multilingual Publishing Inc.; Mario Ciccoritti, proprietor
SIZE: Medium
SPECIAL SERVICES: Special orders
SPECIAL EVENTS: N/A
GETTING THERE: Parking in front of the store

Coming into Librital Book Centre you might think you had entered the stacks of an Italian university library and, in fact, the store supplies books to libraries and other institutions all over Canada. High bookcases run down the centre of the store and additional shelves line the walls. Beautiful multivolume editions of Italian literature sit beside Italian translations of the English classics (there are three different editions of *Moby Dick* in Italian, followed by translations of Pushkin, Maupassant, Schiller, and Hugo). There are many different kinds of dictionaries — technical, business, medical, commercial, French Italian, Italian Spanish, Italian Greek, and such specialized reference works as a *Dizionario dei proverbi Italiani*. The collection includes scholarly works on aesthetics, art, Greek and Latin classics, history, literary criticism, literature, music (e.g., *Tutti i libretti di Mozart*), philosophy, and political science, as well as children's books with cassettes, cookbooks, and Italian fiction.

LICHTMAN'S NEWS AND BOOKS

Head Office: 24 Ryerson Avenue,
Suite 400
Toronto, Ontario M5T 2P3
416-703-7773 (FAX 416-703-1078)

SPECIALTY: General books and newspapers
OWNER: Corporation
SIZE: Medium
SPECIAL SERVICES: Special orders, book club discounts
SPECIAL EVENTS: Canadian author book signings
GETTING THERE: Most stores are on the Yonge subway line

Lichtman's is a friendly, attractive chain carrying popular fiction and non-fiction. Major categories include art, beauty, books on tape, business and computer, child care, decorating, dogs, food and drink, gardening, health, history, mystery, poetry, reference, science, science fiction, sports, and travel. Most of the stores have a substantial section devoted to children's books and books for young people. You will also find over two hundred fifty newspapers and over three thousand magazines. Lichtman's maintains an extensive backlist, specializing in more obscure titles. There are outlets at Atrium on Bay, 595 Bay Street (416-591-1617); Yonge & Richmond, 144 Yonge Street (416-368-7390); Yonge & Bloor, 842 Yonge Street (416-924-4186); Yonge & Eglinton, 2299 Yonge Street (416-482-2462); Yonge & St. Clair, 1430 Yonge Street (416-922-7271); Bayview Village, 2901 Bayview Avenue (416-221-5216); The Promenade, 1 Promenade Circle, Thornhill (905-881-5488); and Yorkdale Shopping Centre, 3401 Dufferin Street (416-783-9723).

THE LION, THE WITCH AND THE WARDROBE

888 Eglinton Avenue West
(near Bathurst)
Toronto, Ontario M6C 2B6
416-785-9177 (NO FAX)

SPECIALTY: Children's books
OWNER: Linda Spiegel
SIZE: Small
SPECIAL SERVICES: Special orders, teachers' discounts, orders for teachers and school libraries; book club (buy 12, next is free)
SPECIAL EVENTS: Author signings (illustrators of children's books occasionally do demonstrations)
GETTING THERE: Eglinton West bus from Yonge and Eglinton; parking on street

A huge lion on the sidewalk draws attention to an attractive bookshop decorated with stuffed figures of Franklin the Turtle, Madeline, Babar the Elephant, Curious George, and other literary personages. The books are displayed in a variety of styles, some propped up on horizontal surfaces, others in rotating exhibits, others on shelves set at interesting angles. The collection is divided roughly by age into ABC/123, Pre-School, I'm Reading, and Active Readers. In addition to books, the store carries audio cassettes, crafts, and puzzles. The Lion, the Witch and the Wardrobe is open seven days a week, 9 to 6.

MABEL'S FABLES, THE STORY BOOK STORE

662 Mt. Pleasant Road
(near Eglinton)
Toronto, Ontario M4S 2N3
416-322-0438 (No FAX)

SPECIALTY: Children's books, organized by age group
OWNER: Susan McCullogh and Eleanor LeFave
SIZE: Small
SPECIAL SERVICES: Special orders, baby baskets for newborns sent by courrier
SPECIAL EVENTS: Story time each Wednesday at 10:30 a.m.
GETTING THERE: Eglinton subway station, then bus to Mt. Pleasant; parking on street

In our visits we have encountered many bookstore cats, but the Mabel of Mabel's Fables is the first to have given her name to the store, though it may take you a while to find Mabel amid the kaleidoscopic decorative detail. Numbered lampshades indicate age groups from "Baby" to "12," and an attached card gives "Top 10" lists for each group. There is a pink-and-white park bench for small readers to sit on, stuffed animals, and a collection of dolls. A huge stuffed elephant occupies a nook near the ceiling. The staff specializes in personal service. ("When a teacher asks for books with a pirate theme, we can give her *Grandma and the Pirates* and ten others.") In addition to its two bookstores, both wheelchair accessible, Mabel's Fables organizes shop-at-home parties, publishes a newsletter called *Spread the Word*, sponsors the "Spread the Word to Sick Kids" program, and sells Mabel's Fables Loot Bags. Another store is located at 2939 Bloor Street West (near the Royal York subway station; 416-233-8830). Its cat is named "Fable."

MAISON DE LA PRESSE INTERNATIONALE

124 Yorkville Avenue
(near Hazelton)
Toronto, Ontario M5R 1C2
416-928-2328 (no FAX)

SPECIALTY: French-language books; magazines and newspapers from all over the world
OWNER: Hachette Corporation; Joe Murta, manager
SIZE: Small
SPECIAL SERVICES: Special orders, orders for immersion schools, etc.
SPECIAL EVENTS: N/A
GETTING THERE: Bay station on Bloor subway line; parking lots nearby

Maison de la Presse Internationale carries between 2,500 and 3,000 different serials, including a large number of academic journals as well as popular magazines in Spanish, Italian, German, French, and English. There are also around 100 international newspapers. The store carries paperbound editions of French literature classics (both in French and in English translation) as well as French translations of English literature. One also finds children's books in French, French dictionaries, French-language student travel guides and — that uniquely French art-form — hardcover comics, both in the original French and in English translation. The staff all speak French and English.

THE MAP ROOM AT EXPLORATION HOUSE

18 Birch Avenue (south of Summerhill)
Toronto, Ontario M4V 1C8
416-922-5153 (No fax)

SPECIALTY: Antiquarian and reference books on art, nature, early voyages, etc.
OWNER: Liana Sneyd
SIZE: Small
SPECIAL SERVICES: Mail order
SPECIAL EVENTS: N/A
GETTING THERE: Summerhill subway station on the Yonge line; street parking

Exploration House encompasses The Map Room, The Wildlife Gallery, The Sporting Art Gallery, and The Marine Arts Gallery. Under these main thematic headings, Exploration House features 15th- to 19th-century antique maps and charts of Canada, the world, and the heavens; early globes; scientific and marine instruments; Arctic art and artifacts; scrimshaw; fine marine paintings and prints; animal, sporting, botanical, landscape, historical, topographical, architectural and ornamental art; old ship models; and important documents. The select, if small, collection of antiquarian books concentrates on early voyages, exploration and discovery, the Arctic, architecture, and the arts and sciences.

A flyer about Exploration House, quoting the famous jeweller Louis Cartier, captures the spirit of antiquarian book collecting: "You can always make more money; but if you miss this gem you will never get another like it, for it is unique!"

MASTERMIND EDUCATIONAL

Head Office: 465 Milner Avenue
Toronto, Ontario M1B 2K4
416-321-8984 (FAX 416-321-8988)

SPECIALTY: Children's books, activities, toys
OWNER: Mastermind Educational
SIZE: Small
SPECIAL SERVICES: Special orders
SPECIAL EVENTS: Character visits

Primarily a toy store with an emphasis on arts and crafts and software, Mastermind Educational stocks a small but judicious selection of children's story books, activity books, and books designed to stimulate a child's imagination, such as the Usborne Young Puzzle Books, which combine stories with picture puzzles. Of particular interest is the branch at the Ontario Science Centre, soon to be considerably expanded. Here, in place of arts and crafts, one finds science-oriented toys and books focusing on experiments and introductions to scientific topics. Adults may be interested in books of puzzles, and essays on the philosophy of science. The collection aims at covering the most interesting and sophisticated topics of contemporary science in language accessible to the lay reader. The staff are generally knowledgeable and helpful.

Locations in Toronto include 3350 Yonge Street (416-487-7177), the largest store in the chain; 4242 Dundas Street West (416-239-1600); 1947 Queen Street East (416-699-3797); and the Ontario Science Centre, 770 Don Mills Road (416-422-0434). Additional branches may be found in Aurora, Markham, Mississauga, and Pickering.

MATANA JUDAICA

248 Steeles Avenue West, Unit 6
(at Hilda)
Thornhill, Ontario L4J 1A1
905-731-6543 (FAX 905-882-6196)

SPECIALTY: Judaica
OWNER: Riva Green
SIZE: Small
SPECIAL SERVICES: Special orders for weddings, Hippah orders, marriage contracts
SPECIAL EVENTS: Book signings
GETTING THERE: Steeles bus; parking in plaza

Bright colours, upbeat music, elaborately decorated wedding contracts, and a friendly staff combine to make Matana Judaica a particularly happy store. The small collection includes children's storybooks, crafts and colouring books in English and Hebrew, Bibles and prayerbooks in different styles, books of commentary and instruction in Jewish religious practices, kosher cookbooks, and coffee-table books on Jewish history, music, theatre, art and traditions, as well as gifts, cassettes, and religious articles. In a striking example of cultural exchange, the store carries a series of twelve video cassettes, entitled *Shalom Sesame*, in which familiar Sesame Street characters present aspects of Jewish life and holidays and tour a number of Israeli cities.

McBURNIE AND CUTLER

698 Queen Street West
(near Bathurst)
Toronto, Ontario M6J 1E7
416-504-8873 (FAX 416-504-8418)

SPECIALTY: Used books specializing in music and Canadiana, some antiquarian books and remainders
OWNER: Michael McBurnie and Tina Cutler
SIZE: Large
SPECIAL SERVICES: Occasional catalogue
SPECIAL EVENTS: N/A
GETTING THERE: Queen Street streetcar; metered parking on street

McBurnie and Cutler is a large, serious, used bookstore carrying mostly hardbound books. General readers will find books on Canadian history, Canadian art, English history, film, law, military history, science, Toronto and local histories, and true crime. The store has a strong music section, with seven bookcases, offering such titles as the 4th edition (1939) of *Grove's Dictionary of Music* as well as very up-to-date books in the field. A large section on literature encompasses a number of first editions along with the old Modern Library and Franklin Library editions. Readers looking for a solid used bookstore with a substantial stock will be rewarded by a visit here.

MODERN BOOKS AND RECORDS

494 Dundas Street West
(near Spadina)
Toronto, Ontario M5T 1G9
416-979-1365 (FAX 416-733-1083)

SPECIALTY: Chinese books
OWNER: Robert Lee
SIZE: Small
SPECIAL SERVICES: N/A
SPECIAL EVENTS: N/A
GETTING THERE: Spadina bus or Dundas streetcar;
    parking on street

Modern Books and Records is one of a number of bookstores serving Toronto's substantial Chinese community. These bookstores, serving an almost exclusively Chinese-speaking clientele, tend to provide labels and other information only in Chinese. My bilingual assistants indicated that the small collection includes books in a variety of categories: automobile maintenance, biography, business (marketing and management), children's books (including calligraphy for children), child care, Chinese opera, Chinese philosophy, classical poetry, cookbooks, dictionaries, fitness for women, health and medicine, I.Q. tests, interior design, language, modern poetry and literature, music, novels, parapsychology, politics and history, religion (Buddhism), sports, and women's studies. In addition, there are a number of outdated computer manuals as well as cassettes for learning Mandarin, Cantonese, and English.

MOYER'S, KIDS ARE WORTH IT, AND MOYER'S LEARNING WORLD INC.

Head Office: 25 Milvan Drive
Toronto, Ontario M9L 1Z1
416-749-2222 (FAX 416-749-8640)

SPECIALTY: Children's books, crafts, toys, teacher's
    supplies
OWNER: Moyer's Learning World Group
SIZE: Small to medium (average store size in
    Canada is 2,000 sq. ft.; 136 stores in 7 countries)
SPECIAL SERVICES: Special orders
SPECIAL EVENTS: Regular activities: June–July
    included hula hoop contest, skipping rope contest,
    embroidering floss, Father's Day card making,
    storytelling, lemonade stand, T-shirt painting

Moyer's, Kids Are Worth It has everything that primary school teachers and parents could want for an active, colourful classroom. There are reading and writing workbooks, activity books, junior dictionaries, drills, colouring books; books on geography, Canadian history, holiday projects and enhancing self-esteem; teaching units on oceans, soil, birds, jungles, and Native Americans, as well as literature notes which include puzzles, games, and critical thinking activities. In addition, teachers can find stickers, name tags, flash cards, math games, rubber animals, bulletin board posters, poster paints, decorations, science materials, clip art, charts, modelling clay, and all manner of kits.

Branches in the Metro area include Bayview Village (416-223-8787), Malvern Town Centre (416-297-0344), Newtonbrook (416-225-6584), Fairview Mall (416-490-0040), Woodbine Centre (416-674-5677), Yorkdale Shopping Centre (416-256-7206), and Erin Mills Town Centre (905-828-9424).

MUSEUM FOR TEXTILES

55 Centre Avenue
Toronto, Ontario M5G 2H5
416-599-5321

THE MUSIC BOOK STORE

122 Laird Drive, 2nd Floor
(off Eglinton, east of Bayview)
Toronto, Ontario M4G 3V3
416-696-2850 or 1-800-654-1454
(FAX 416-696-0736)
e-mail: musicbk@passport.ca
http://www.scinet.com/~musicbk/

SPECIALTY: Ethnographic textiles, folk weaving, rugs
OWNER: Museum for Textiles
SIZE: Very small (400 titles)
SPECIAL SERVICES: Exhibition catalogues of the Museum for Textiles
SPECIAL EVENTS: N/A
GETTING THERE: St. Patrick subway station; pay parking lot next door

SPECIALTY: New and used books on music, biographies, histories, and sheet music
OWNER: Manfred Koch
SIZE: Small
SPECIAL SERVICES: Special orders, mail orders, book searches
SPECIAL EVENTS: Occasional live music, especially during the summer
GETTING THERE: Leaside #56 bus from Eglinton station or Donlands station; parking behind store

This small but distinctive book collection occupies a tiny corner of the museum's second-floor gift shop and, like the museum itself, is devoted entirely to textiles. Although there are a few "how-to" books for the avid needleworker or quilter, most are art historical in nature, describing aspects of the history and technology of textiles, beading, oriental carpets of many kinds, or historical and contemporary textiles from different parts of the world. Nearly all the works are heavily illustrated. The store also sells those titles pertaining to textiles from the inexpensive *Shire* paperback series from Great Britain, giving concise historical overviews of the textile industry. Volunteer staffing.

As the name suggests, The Music Book Store specializes in books on music, including music history, ethnomusicology and biography, books on instruments, opera, and the music business. It carries academic as well as popular books in these areas and, while a particular title may be out of stock, you will probably find a book that covers your area of interest. The jazz collection, by contrast, attempts complete coverage of the field, and indeed the chances are very good of finding a given book. The jazz section draws collectors from the entire city. The store also carries sheet music, piano music, anthologies of Broadway music, and cassette tapes. Booklists are periodically published.

THE NAUTICAL MIND

Radisson Plaza Hotel,
249 Queens Quay West (near Rees)
Toronto, Ontario M5J 2N5
416-203-1163 (FAX 416-203-0729)
e-mail: books@nauticalmind.com
http://www.nauticalmind.com

SPECIALTY: Nautical books and marine charts
OWNER: Dorothy LeBaron and Ross Wilson
SIZE: Small (4,000 titles)
SPECIAL SERVICES: Catalogues, mail orders anywhere in the world
SPECIAL EVENTS: International speaker series in fall and early winter
GETTING THERE: LRT streetcar from Union subway station to Rees Street; 15-minute parking just outside store; lots nearby

The Nautical Mind can supply everything from videos and sailing simulator software for the armchair sailor to marine charts for the serious helmsman planning a voyage from Lake Ontario via intercoastal waterways down to the Bahamas, or anywhere on the globe. Their annotated, illustrated catalogue, *The Nautical Mind Reference Book of Nautical Titles*, lists 1,800 books. The collection includes books on art and artists, boat construction, cruising, design, electricity/electronics, engines, fiction, Great Lakes, knots, lines, maintenance, maps, multihulls, photography, racing, seamanship, small boats, and voyages. The walls are covered with framed pictures of ships ancient and modern, canoes and kayaks, while from the store windows you can see pleasure boats and a view of the Toronto Islands. The store is open seven days a week.

NEGEV BOOK AND GIFT STORE

3509 Bathurst Street
(between Lawrence and Wilson)
Toronto, Ontario M6A 2C5
416-781-9356 (FAX 416-781-0071)

SPECIALTY: Jewish books and Judaica
OWNER: Arthur Kaplan and Morty Kaplan
SIZE: Medium (10,000 books)
SPECIAL SERVICES: Mail orders, special orders
SPECIAL EVENTS: N/A
GETTING THERE: Spadina subway to Lawrence West, then Lawrence bus; parking in plaza

Negev Book and Gift Store offers a large, well-organized collection serving the Jewish community. There are handsomely bound multivolume sets of Jewish law, dictionaries (English/Yiddish and English/Hebrew), Hebrew grammars and other learning aids, Bibles and Bible commentaries. Eight bookcases devoted to children's books include Hebrew alphabet colouring books and Mitzvah projects for the Bar/Bat-Mitzvah. The store also carries titles in ancient history, biography, cookbooks, current affairs, Holocaust, Israel, mysticism, and philosophy, as well as coffee-table books such as *A Day in the Life of Israel* and *Living Traditions: A Celebration of Jewish Life*. Many remainder books are available at substantial savings. In addition to books, the store carries CDs, cassettes, gifts, religious articles, cards, and sing-along books.

NEW AGE BOOKS FOR TRANSFORMATIONAL LIVING

9275 Highway 48
(Sunkist Plaza, at 16th Avenue)
Markham, Ontario L6E 1A1
905-294-3771 (FAX 905-294-3775)

SPECIALTY: New Age books, books for transformational living (spirituality, self-development)
OWNER: Collective
SIZE: Small
SPECIAL SERVICES: Special orders, mail orders, classes and workshops, therapeutic sessions
SPECIAL EVENTS: See below
GETTING THERE: Free parking in plaza

New Age Books serves as an information centre for personal development activities throughout the Metro area. One corner of the store contains dozens of brochures, newsletters, posters, booklets, and business cards for those working in this area, as well as a list of ongoing activities at the store itself: Monday: spiritual healing, intuitive consultation, ear candling, Reiki, Tuesday: astrology, spiritual and soul purpose readings; Friday: Angel listenings. Other services, such as polarity, shiatsu, and reflexology, available by appointment only. The store carries books on addictions, astrology, channelling, cookbooks, death — reincarnation — Edgar Cayce, divination — crystals — dreams, healing and health, meditation and Eastern teachings, reflections, relationships, and prosperity (e.g., *Feel and Grow Rich*; *Think and Grow Rich*; *Your Infinite Power to Be Rich*). You can also find candles, incense, aromatherapy oils, posters, and videos, jewellery, angel gifts, tapes and CDs, clothing, magazines, native crafts, health and herbal products, and original intuitive artwork.

NEW BALLENFORD BOOKS

600 Markham Street
(near Bloor and Bathurst)
Toronto, Ontario M6G 2L8
416-588-0800 (FAX 416-588-1166)

SPECIALTY: Architecture, interior design, gardens and garden history, urbanism
OWNER: A group of architects
SIZE: Small
SPECIAL SERVICES: Mail orders, special orders
SPECIAL EVENTS: Exhibitions of drawings by architects, book launches
GETTING THERE: Cumberland subway station; parking lots nearby

New Ballenford Books serves professional architects and the general public with hardbound, high-quality books on architecture, interior design, gardens, and related subjects. One can find such titles as *The Works of Christopher Wren*, *Art and Architecture of the Middle Ages*, *The Bavarian Rococo School*, *The House Restorer's Guide*, *Gardens of the French Riviera*, *Private Gardens of London*, *Landmarks of Soviet Architecture 1917–1991*, and *Frank Lloyd Wright: The Lost Years, 1910–1922*. An entire wall of the store is devoted to exhibiting architectural drawings.

NEW ERA COMICS

287 Bridgeland Avenue, Unit 2
(near Dufferin and Highway 401)
North York, Ontario M6A 1Z4
416-784-9376 (FAX 416-512-1520)

SPECIALTY: Comics, cards, games, Magic games, and non-sport cards
OWNER: Leo Domenic
SIZE: Small
SPECIAL SERVICES: N/A
SPECIAL EVENTS: Card and comics shows 8–4 on weekends; end-of-month sales
GETTING THERE: Lansdowne bus #47B from Lansdowne subway station; parking in front of store

New Era Comics carries around 200 current titles in the main room of the store, with a separate room containing bins of back issues. One will find the usual publications by DC, Marvel, and Image comics, but collectors seek out the store particularly for its stock of comics by independent small presses including Antarctic Press, Blackout, Calibre (Kabuki), Chaos, Crusade, Cyrus (Dawn and Fang), Entity, Harris, Immortelle, Lightning Comics (Hellina), and London Nights (Razar).

NEW WORLD BOOKSTORE

442 Dundas Street West
(near Huron)
Toronto, Ontario M5T 1G7
416-977-6029 (No FAX)

SPECIALTY: Chinese books
OWNER: Tommy Lai
SIZE: Small
SPECIAL SERVICES: N/A
SPECIAL EVENTS: N/A
GETTING THERE: Dundas streetcar; parking on street

The New World Bookstore is one of a handful of bookstores in the Dundas/Spadina area specializing in Chinese books. These bookstores generally carry videos, magazines, and newspapers in addition to books, and the bulk of their trade often comes from these former activities with the result that the turnover in the book section remains low. Considerable discounts are frequently available on books which sell for considerably more in the modern emporiums of Scarborough and Markham. Categories (none labelled) include biography, business, Chinese literature, fashion (rather outdated), fictionalized treatments of history, general interest, health, history, legendaries (romances with mythic heroes), medicine, music, out-of-date computer books, parapsychology (fortune-telling), religion, sex, short stories, and a variety of dictionaries (English-Chinese, Japanese-Chinese, English-Vietnamese).

NICHOLAS HOARE

45 Front Street East
(near Church)
Toronto, Ontario M5E 1B3
416-777-2665 (FAX 416-777-0295)

SPECIALTY: A high-quality general collection with an emphasis on British books

OWNER: Nicholas Hoare

SIZE: Medium (15,000 titles in stock)

SPECIAL SERVICES: One of the best special-ordering services in the city due to the connection with Hoare's library wholesaling business (turnaround in as little as 48 hours)

SPECIAL EVENTS: Book launches (receptions for the news media and the professional community); site of announcement of short-list of the Governor General's Award; host for world literacy series

GETTING THERE: Union Station or King subway station on Yonge line; metered parking on Front Street

Nicholas Hoare has recreated an old-style European bookstore in a refurbished historic building in Toronto's theatre district. With polished wooden floors and shelves, brass railings, and ladders reaching to the upper sections, the Nicholas Hoare bookstore merits a visit just for the pleasure of experiencing its unique ambience. We all love to curl up with a good book, but seldom have the opportunity to do so in a bookstore. Nicholas Hoare offers comfortable armchairs in front of a blazing fire and a wide selection of reading matter. The bookstore has a strong collection in 20th-century literature, and a large selection of children's books. The store professes to have quality as its specialty, and an inspection of the collection bears out the claim. This is indeed a bookstore for the discriminating reader.

THE OCCULT SHOP

109 Vaughan Road
(north of St. Clair, west of Bathurst)
Toronto, Ontario M6C 2L9
416-787-4043 (No FAX)

SPECIALTY: Occult and metaphysical subjects

OWNER: Richard James

SIZE: Small (3,000 titles)

SPECIAL SERVICES: Mail orders

SPECIAL EVENTS: Psychic readers (palmistry, Tarot cards)

GETTING THERE: Eglinton West subway station on Spadina line; parking on street

Entering The Occult Shop is like walking into a different world. Bottles of incense, oils, and spices line the walls, sprinkling salts, inks, and handmade incense sticks and canes fill a number of shelves, a large collection of medicinal herbs occupy bins and tables, and a full-colour tarot display represents the shop's entire selection of cards. The Occult Shop carries books on astral trails, auras, crystals, dreams, health, miscellaneous divination, Native Americans, New Age, Norse runes, numerology, paganism, palmistry, psychic sciences, psychology, Tarot, western magic, wicca, women's spirituality, as well as Celtic, Egyptian, and Greek mythologies. The store also sells silver and gold jewellery in pagan and Celtic designs as well as swords, daggers, scrying mirrors, crystal balls, and ceramic figurines. A jar at the counter invites contributions to The Wicca Church of Canada.

THE OMEGA CENTRE

29 Yorkville Avenue
(near Yonge and Bloor)
Toronto, Ontario M4W 1L1
416-975-9086 (FAX 416-975-0731)

SPECIALTY: A bookstore devoted to self-discovery

OWNER: Corporation; Mary-Anne Solski, managing director

SIZE: Medium (15,000 titles)

SPECIAL SERVICES: Special orders, conference rooms for meetings

SPECIAL EVENTS: Calendar lists nightly activities

GETTING THERE: Bloor/Yonge subway station; parking in nearby lots

The Omega Centre has become a focal point for New Age modes of self-discovery. The store's calendar of events contains advertisements for advanced energy healing, craniosacral therapy, deep trance channelling, energy balancing, experiential workshops, Feng Shui consultation, hypnotherapy, inner guidance through Eckankar, intensive soul fragment integration, Japanese acupuncture, karmic astrology, Kriya Yoga meditation, light body integration, and moxibustion. The store carries books on acupuncture, aromatherapy, breath therapy, clairvoyance, graphology, homeopathy, iridology, massage, mythology, North American Indian traditions, palmistry, pendulum, rebirthing, reflexology, reincarnation, rolfing, runes, Tarot, wicca magic, and yoga as well as crystals, inspirational tapes, and many New Age journals.

ONE MORE TIME BOOKS

462 Parliament Street (near Carlton)
Toronto, Ontario M5A 3A2
416-968-7801 (No FAX)

SPECIALTY: Pocketbooks bought, sold, and traded

OWNER: Denise Redwood

SIZE: Medium (12,000 books)

SPECIAL SERVICES: Book searches

SPECIAL EVENTS: N/A

GETTING THERE: Carlton Street streetcar; parking on street

One More Time Books is located in historic Old Cabbagetown, a neighbourhood worth a visit for its own sake. Its neighbours include Lennie's Whole Foods, Neat Stuff, Spinning Wheels (a bicycle store), and Tribal Arts and Crafts. As a neighbourhood bookstore, One More Time contains, according to its owner, "an exhaustive range of paperbacks, cleaned and alphabetically organized." The store offers substantial discounts on new and remainder books, coffee-table books, children's books and cookbooks, and a fair number of good trade paperbacks. Those just looking for something to read and relax will find pocketbook best-sellers, classics, mystery, science fiction, self-help, suspense, war, and westerns.

OPEN AIR BOOKS AND MAPS

25 Toronto Street (lower level,
near Yonge and Adelaide)
Toronto, Ontario M5C 2R1
416-363-0719 (No FAX)

SPECIALTY: Nature, travel, and outdoor books and maps
OWNER: Jeff Axler
SIZE: Medium (17,000 titles)
SPECIAL SERVICES: Mail orders
SPECIAL EVENTS: N/A
GETTING THERE: King subway station; nearby parking lots; the shop is located down a set of stairs, just beneath Druxy's delicatessen

Open Air Books and Maps is the place to come for road maps, country maps, city maps, and regional maps. It offers an astonishing collection of books and travel guides crammed into a small, underground store. One finds books on Africa, Asia, astronomy, birds, Canada, canoeing, climbing, ecology, hiking, India, Latin America, mammals, Northern Europe, Out West, reference, South Pacific, United Kingdom, as well as bed-and-breakfast guides to every place imaginable. Open Air Books caters particularly to those whose travels are oriented around activities, from bird-watching to kayaking to serious mountaineering. Open Air offers capsule histories, cultural backgrounds, myths and legends, current events, and literary travel accounts to complement its extensive guidebook selection.

OPEN CITY

1374 Danforth Avenue
(near Monarch Park)
Toronto, Ontario M4J 1M9
416-461-8087 (No FAX)

SPECIALTY: Used books, records and CDs
OWNER: Steve Wright
SIZE: Medium
SPECIAL SERVICES: N/A
SPECIAL EVENTS: N/A
GETTING THERE: Greenwood or Coxwell subway station on Bloor line; metered parking in front of store

Open City is a used bookstore occupying two floors and offering both paperback and hardbound books on fiction, history, music, occult, poetry, science fiction and fantasy, suspense and mystery, theatre, TV and movies, along with a large selection of used popular, classical, and jazz LP records, cassettes, and compact discs.

PAGES BOOKS AND MAGAZINES

256 Queen Street West
(near John)
Toronto, Ontario M5V 1Z8
416-598-1447 (FAX 416-598-2042)

SPECIALTY: Fiction, cultural theory, film studies, gender studies
OWNER: Marc and Steve Glassman
SIZE: Medium
SPECIAL SERVICES: Special orders, including books from academic presses
SPECIAL EVENTS: sell tickets for and support non-profit events
GETTING THERE: Osgoode subway station or Queen Street streetcar; parking on street

Pages Books and Magazines specializes in books on cultural theory and literary small press publications. It is also a general bookstore with a difference — trade paperbacks rather than mass-market, and books on the arts, contemporary philosophy, and high technology rather than best-sellers. In short, Pages caters to the special needs of a unique neighbourhood. Queen Street West, once the home of Toronto's arts community, has now become a diverse spectrum of alternative lifestyles. An open-air crafts market, street musicians, and vendors selling jewellery stand near shops specializing in items as diverse as crystals or condoms. In Pages Books and Magazines, the best-selling magazine is *Wired*. The science section carries books on chaos, fuzzy logic, mapping the mind, and cognitive theory. Book categories include art and literary criticism, biography, children, cooking, film, gay and lesbian studies, health and sports, humour, literature, lively arts, mystery, New Age, philosophy, religion, photography, poetry, reference, science and technology, small press, social studies, and video. There are also sections devoted to women's studies and to First Nations.

PANNONIA BOOKS — THE HUNGARIAN BOOK STORE

344 Bloor Street West, Suite 509
(near Spadina)
Toronto, Ontario M5S 1W9
416-966-5156 (FAX same)
e-mail: pannonia@interlog.com
http://www.panbooks.com

SPECIALTY: New and used Hungarian books
OWNER: Mrs. Kate Karácsony
SIZE: Small
SPECIAL SERVICES: Mail order
SPECIAL EVENTS: N/A
GETTING THERE: Spadina subway station; parking on street

Pannonia Books carries publications in Hungarian, English translations of Hungarian books, and Hungarian translations of English best-sellers. (Agatha Christie, Ken Follett, and Danielle Steel are very popular in Hungary.) The stock changes regularly depending on the availability of books from Hungary, but the standard categories include art, children's books, cookbooks, dictionaries, history, lexicons, literature, philosophy, poetry, and religion. The tiny store, essentially a small, book-lined vault, also contains a twenty-volume encyclopedia and the nearly complete works of Jokai Mor in 120 volumes, with more on the way. The store also carries music tapes and CDs and more than fifty Hungarian magazines and newspapers. There are numerous Hungarian restaurants in the neighbourhood.

PAPERGRAFIX

1708 Avenue Road
(near Fairlawn)
Toronto, Ontario M4M 3Y6
416-781-6300 (FAX 416-781-7489)

SPECIALTY: General
OWNER: Sandra Shleifman
SIZE: Small
SPECIAL SERVICES: Special orders
SPECIAL EVENTS: N/A
GETTING THERE: Lawrence subway station and bus or York Mills subway and Wilson bus; parking on street

As the name implies, the main emphasis of Papergrafix is on paper and stationery. A good neighbourhood bookstore, Papergrafix has strengths in cooking, gardening, interior decorating, self-help, and children's books. This is not an all-inclusive store, but the small stock represents intelligent, tasteful selections in its areas of specialization.

PARADISE CARDS AND COMICS

3278 Yonge Street
(north of Lawrence)
Toronto, Ontario M4N 2M6
416-487-9807 (FAX 416-322-4852)

SPECIALTY: Buying and selling Golden and Silver Age comics, new releases, gaming, Magic cards, figures
OWNER: Peter Dixon
SIZE: Large (100,000 comics in a 1,000-square-foot store)
SPECIAL SERVICES: Membership, want lists, layaway plans
SPECIAL EVENTS: Quarterly store sales, Magic tournaments
GETTING THERE: 4 blocks north of Lawrence subway station; parking on street

The so-called Silver Age of super-hero comic books, roughly 1950 to 1970, marks the domain of many serious comic book collectors, who will pay up to $8,500 for *Spiderman* #1 (1962). Paradise Comics carries one of the larger Silver Age collections in the city, along with movie comics, collectible figurines, gaming materials, and Magic cards. Under "S," I found *Sandman, Savage Dragon, Savage She Hulk, Second Defender, Solar, Spectre, Spirits of Vengeance, Static, Stormwatch,* and *Supreme,* in addition to the more familiar entries.

PARENTBOOKS

201 Harbord Street
(near Bathurst)
Toronto, Ontario M5S 1H6
416-537-8334 (FAX 416-537-9499)

SPECIALTY: Parenting, pregnancy, and related topics
OWNER: Patti Kirk and Bill Elleker
SIZE: Medium (14,000 titles)
SPECIAL SERVICES: Mail orders, special orders, bibliographies, booklists
SPECIAL EVENTS: Book launches
GETTING THERE: Close to Bathurst subway station on the Bloor line; parking on Harbord Street until 4 p.m.

For most of us, parenting is a learned skill, and Parentbooks offers a multitude of books to assist parents in such areas as resolving conflicts, building their child's self-esteem, choosing daycare, and helping with homework. In addition to parents, the store serves schools, community groups, and professional counselors with books on adoption, child abuse, child and adolescent therapy, childbirth, divorce, fertility and infertility, grief and loss, health and safety, infants, nutrition, special needs, and violence against women. For assistance, one may consult the free bibliographies and salespeople with expertise in various areas of parenting. There is an attractive collection of children's books as well as toys for children to play with while their parents browse.

PATHFINDER BOOK STORE

827 Bloor Street West
(east of Ossington)
Toronto, Ontario M6G 1M1
416-533-4324 (FAX same)

SPECIALTY: Socialism, Marxism, revolutionary leaders
OWNER: Toronto Social Science and Education Society
SIZE: Small (300 titles published by the Pathfinder Press)
SPECIAL SERVICES: Annual catalogue, mail orders, special orders, Pathfinder Readers Club discounts
SPECIAL EVENTS: Militant Labour Forum headquarters
GETTING THERE: Ossington subway station on Bloor line; parking on street

The Pathfinder Book Store serves as a focal point for the militant labour movement, as reflected in its section titles: Art, Culture and Politics; Black Rights and the Fight Against Racism; The Cuban Revolution in World Politics; Introduction to Socialism; New International; Scientific View of History, Politics and Economics; Struggles of Working Farmers; Struggles of Native People; Trade Unions: Their Past, Present and Future; Women's Rights: Issues in the Struggle. Other sections are divided geographically into areas of the Third World (Africa, Middle East, Asia, Latin America, the Caribbean) or by revolutionary leaders (Engels, Lenin, Marx, Trotsky). The Pathfinder Book Store also distributes three newspapers: *The Militant*, *Perspectiva Mundial* (in Spanish), and *Granma* (a Cuban newspaper published in English and Spanish).

PAULINE BOOKS AND MEDIA

3022 Dufferin Street
(south of Lawrence)
Toronto, Ontario M6B 3T5
416-781-9131 or 1-800-668-2078
(FAX 416-783-1615)

SPECIALTY: Religious books in English, Italian, and Spanish, Christian tapes and videos
OWNER: Daughters of St. Paul Community
SIZE: Medium (22,000 titles)
SPECIAL SERVICES: Book consignments for parishes, video rentals, textbooks for schools and university courses, seminars in schools on Christian music and values
SPECIAL EVENTS: Indoor sale before Christmas with instrumentalists and singers
GETTING THERE: Lawrence West subway station; parking in front of and behind store

A religious sister or lay staff member is available to answer questions at the information desk while large display signs indicate the individual sections in this well laid out store. "Spirituality" occupies nine bookcases and there is quite an extensive foreign language section. Other categories include biographies, charismatic, children's liturgy, children's religious books, church documents, family life, homiletics, liturgy, marriage preparation, prayerbooks, psychology, religious education resources, scripture, seasonal, sociology, theology/philosophy/ethics, and writings of saints. A separate children's room includes figures from Noah's Ark and a box of stuffed animals to play with or, for the more bellicose, a Nintendo game, Joshua: Battle of Jericho. A third department displays cassettes, videos (both for rental and purchase), and CDs. A new product line for the store is software.

PENDRAGON COMICS AND CARDS

3759 Lakeshore Boulevard West
(near Kipling)
Toronto, Ontario M8W 1R1
416-253-6974 (No FAX)

SPECIALTY: New and old comics, especially Silver Age, videos, gaming, paperbacks related to gaming or comics
OWNER: Darcy
SIZE: Medium (20,000 new and old comics)
SPECIAL SERVICES: Reserving, memberships, recommendations to readers
SPECIAL EVENTS: N/A
GETTING THERE: Long Branch GO train; parking in mall

Pendragon Comics claims to have more Silver Age (classic 1960s) comics than any other store in Toronto. An elaborate reservation system, with cubbyholes for individual customers, draws customers from other Ontario cities. In addition to mainline comics, new and old, the store carries items from a number of large and small independent publishers including Atomeka, Caliber, Continuity, Claypool, Eternity, Innovation, Millenium, Now, Tundra, and others. Under "S" I found *Stormwatch, Static, Saint Sinner, Sandman, Savage Dragon,* and *Shadow Cabinet,* several of which I had not noticed in other stores. Pendragon Comics is open every day except Canada Day and Christmas. A second store may be found at 1107 Laonene Park Road in Mississauga (905-278-8625).

PEOPLE'S BOOK STORE

418 Dundas Street West
(near Spadina)
Toronto, Ontario M5E 1E9
416-977-8965 (NO FAX)

SPECIALTY: Chinese books
OWNER: Henry Tang
SIZE: Small
SPECIAL SERVICES: N/A
SPECIAL EVENTS: N/A
GETTING THERE: Dundas Street streetcar or
Spadina bus; parking on street

People's Book Store is a well-organized bookstore with titles in both English and Chinese. It offers books in business, child education, cookbooks, fashion, fiction (both romances and legends), history, literature old and new, medicine, opera librettos, parapsychology, photography, poetry, popular music, and science. A large section of dictionaries includes dictionaries of physics, biology, and chemistry as well as French/Chinese, Japanese, and English/Chinese dictionaries. There are also comic books, magazines, and videos for learning Chinese or teaching Cantonese, but no movie videos. A second branch of the store is located at 273 Spadina Avenue (416-596-8709).

THE PIRANHA SHOP

1550 Avenue Road
(north of Lawrence)
Toronto, Ontario M5M 3X5
416-789-3512 (FAX 416-789-9066)

SPECIALTY: Dog books, new and antiquarian;
figurines, modern and rare
OWNER: Paul Wettlauser
SIZE: Medium (over 10,000 titles)
SPECIAL SERVICES: Mail orders, catalogue for
out-of-print books, searches, shipping worldwide
SPECIAL EVENTS: N/A
GETTING THERE: Lawrence bus from Lawrence
subway station; metered parking on street

One enters The Piranha Shop through a maze of figurines, mascots, and commemorative dishes. Passing one aquarium after another contributes to a feeling of being underwater. The passageway opens into a small room containing books on dogs, arranged alphabetically by species: Afghan, Basset Hound, Boxer, Chow Chow, Doberman, Irish Setter, Portuguese Water Dog, Schnauzer, Terriers. As favourite dog breeds vary no less frequently than clothing fashions, out-of-print books may be the only source of information on many breeds. The store carries books on dog obedience and training, works on cats, tropical fish, hamsters, parrots, pythons, rabbits and turtles, as well as thousands of porcelain figurines.

THE PLEASANT BOOKSTORE

656 Eglinton Avenue East
(near Bayview)
Toronto, Ontario M4P 1P1
416-488-5998 (No FAX)

SPECIALTY: Paperback exchange and half-price remainders
OWNER: Mrs. Patricia Mortimer
SIZE: Small
SPECIAL SERVICES: N/A
SPECIAL EVENTS: N/A
GETTING THERE: Eglinton bus; free parking while shopping

Hundreds of mass-market paperbacks testify to the usefulness of a used book store. The Pleasant Bookstore offers 15% credit for your paperbacks and sells theirs at half price. One can browse easily among books displayed face forward, or on their sides with the spines out. In additional to the usual fare, the store carries a good collection of children's books, attractively displayed. Since kids often outgrow books, like clothes, long before they're worn out, an exchange store makes sense, and The Pleasant Bookstore enjoys a rapid turnover in stock. The store also offers new books at discounted prices. I saw the *Penguin Rhyming Dictionary* in hardcover at $14.99 instead of the regular price of $35.

PORTUGUESE BOOK STORE, INC.

1112 Dundas Street West
(east of Ossington)
Toronto, Ontario M6J 1X2
416-603-7554 or 416-538-0330 (No FAX)

SPECIALTY: Portuguese books and newspapers
OWNER: Privately owned
SIZE: Small
SPECIAL SERVICES: Mail orders, Club do Livro (mails latest books)
SPECIAL EVENTS: N/A
GETTING THERE: Dundas streetcar; parking on street

The Portuguese Book Store is a small store catering to the city's Portuguese community, with fiction and non-fiction in Portuguese and in English translation as well as Portuguese translations of English best-sellers (Jeffrey Archer, Agatha Christie, Graham Greene) or children's classics ranging from Robert Louis Stevenson's *A Ilha do Tesouro* to *Rua Sésamo*. The store carries lots of cookbooks, a variety of dictionaries, including Portuguese Spanish, Portuguese French, and business dictionaries, and aids to recent immigrants such as *English in a Week*. One can also find more than fifty newspapers and magazines, as well as cassettes, videos, and compact discs.

PSYCHIC CENTRE AND BOOK SHOP

2906 Danforth Avenue
(near Victoria Park)
Toronto, Ontario M4C 1M1
416-691-3335 (No FAX)

SPECIALTY: General secondhand bookstore
OWNER: Jackie Lewis
SIZE: Medium (10,000 to 15,000 titles)
SPECIAL SERVICES: N/A
SPECIAL EVENTS: Psychic readings
GETTING THERE: Main Street subway, then Danforth bus or walk from Victoria Park station; parking on street

Psychic readings in the basement seem to be the only overt manifestation of the occult at the Psychic Centre, which offers well-worn paperbacks in a number of categories: arts, biography, business and computers, children, gardening and cooking, horror, mystery, New Age, occult, philosophy, psychology, reference, religion, science fiction and fantasy, science and nature, theatre and poetry, true crime, westerns, women and health.

R.G. MITCHELL FAMILY BOOKS INC.

565 Gordon Baker Road
(near Victoria Park and Steeles)
Willowdale, Ontario M2H 2W2
416-499-2029 (FAX 416-499-6340)

SPECIALTY: Religious books and general topics from a Christian perspective
OWNER: R.G. Mitchell
SIZE: Medium
SPECIAL SERVICES: Special orders, mail orders
SPECIAL EVENTS: Anniversary sale, music night promotions
GETTING THERE: Victoria Park bus to Gordon Baker; parking on premises

R.G. Mitchell Family Books presents a spacious, well-lighted area with carpeted floors and comfortable chairs not just in one corner but throughout the store. There is a pleasant children's toy area enclosed by carpeted stairs. The collection centres on conservative religious texts of an evangelical nature but also includes a number of general topics. Categories include Bibles and Bible commentaries, charismatic interests, children's curriculum, Christian living, cults/New Age/world religions, current issues, devotions, doctrine, evangelism and discipleship, health, language tools, life management, marriage, men/women, music, pastoral aids, reference, self-help, singles, spiritual warfare (countering demon possession), teen non-fiction, teen fiction, and youth ministry.

RED NAILS II

18A Jane Street, lower level
(near Bloor)
Toronto, Ontario M6S 3Y2
416-762-7899 (No FAX)

SPECIALTY: Comic books, role-playing books, graphic novels
OWNER: David Gargaro
SIZE: Small
SPECIAL SERVICES: Memberships (discounts for subscribers), reserve system
SPECIAL EVENTS: N/A
GETTING THERE: Jane subway station; parking on street

Red Nails II is a neighbourhood comic-book store selling primarily standard comics from the 1970s onwards. Issues from the last two months are displayed on racks, the rest in bins. Large comic-book posters hang down in the centre of the store. One may also find a small number of sports cards, manuals and miniatures for role-playing games, graphic novels, and reprints of comic book series *in toto*. A second Red Nails II is located in Sheridan Mall, 1700 Wilson Avenue (telephone 416-242-7899).

RENOUF BOOKS

12 Adelaide Street West
(at Yonge and Adelaide)
Toronto, Ontario M5H 1L6
416-363-3171 (FAX 416-363-5963)
http://fox.nstn.ca/~renouf/

SPECIALTY: Government, international, current affairs, and business publications
OWNER: Gordon Graham
SIZE: Medium
SPECIAL SERVICES: Special orders, mail orders
SPECIAL EVENTS: N/A
GETTING THERE: King subway station; parking at Bay-Adelaide Centre

If you're looking for the complete text of the North American Free Trade Agreement or the latest Royal Commission report, Renouf Books can supply them, as well as documents published by Statistics Canada, OECD, The World Bank, The International Monetary Fund, the World Trade Organization, International Labour Office, UNESCO, United Nations, The Brookings Institute, and many of Canada's leading institutes. The store also carries books on topics of interest to businesses such as computers, environment, finance, law, management, marketing, and a variety of directories. The store publishes a newsletter three times a year, the *RenoufNews*, which highlights new releases, and operates a web site.

ROBERT WRIGHT BOOKS

479 Queen Street West, 2nd Floor
(near Spadina)
Toronto, Ontario M5V 2A9
416-504-2065 (No FAX)

SPECIALTY: Used and rare books on literature and the arts with specialties in modern literature, cinema, Black studies, Pre-Raphaelites, and general antiquarian books
OWNER: Robert Wright
SIZE: Medium
SPECIAL SERVICES: Searches within the field of literature and the arts
SPECIAL EVENTS: N/A
GETTING THERE: Spadina bus to Queen Street or Queen Street streetcar; parking on street

Robert Wright Books occupies two rooms of floor-to-ceiling bookcases neatly arranged like a library. The store caters to both readers and collectors in specific areas. There are five bookcases devoted to cinema, a full bookcase of African-American authors, a large section devoted to the Pre-Raphaelites, William Morris, Ruskin, and the Arts and Crafts Movement, and a substantial section on modern literature, mostly first editions, with an emphasis on Canadian authors. Wright issues catalogues periodically, focusing on modern literature, Canadian literature, mystery, and Latin American literature.

ROYAL ONTARIO MUSEUM BOOKSHOP

110 Queen's Park (Bloor at Avenue Road)
Toronto, Ontario M5S 2C6
416-586-5772 (FAX 416-586-8069)
http://www.rom.on.ca

SPECIALTY: Natural history, science, ancient history
OWNER: Royal Ontario Museum
SIZE: Small (500 titles)
SPECIAL SERVICES: Carries *Rotunda*, the magazine of the Royal Ontario Museum
SPECIAL EVENTS: Occasional author signings by guest lecturers at the museum
GETTING THERE: Museum subway station; parking on Bloor Street

The Royal Ontario Museum lies at the intellectual hub of the city, alongside the University of Toronto and the Royal Conservatory of Music and within sight of Edwards Books & Art and the Bob Miller Book Room. The ROM Bookshop offers nineteenth-century adult games, fine stationery, and a small collection of books focusing on areas of natural science, ancient history, and Canadiana represented in the museum proper. In addition to carrying *Rotunda*, the magazine of the ROM, the bookshop offers publications of the University of Toronto Press bearing the ROM imprint, including the ROM Encounter Series, the ROM Insight Series, and Life Sciences Publications, books not easily found elsewhere. The store also sells catalogues accompanying current and previous museum exhibits.

Across the street, at the Gardiner Museum of Ceramics (111 Queen's Park, Toronto, Ontario M5S 2C7, telephone 416-586-8080), one will find books on glass and china, porcelain, pottery, and related subjects. This collection of fewer than one hundred titles specializes in illustrated histories. Admission to the Gardiner Museum is included with a ticket to the ROM, but both bookshops are accessible without buying a ticket.

THE RYERSON BOOKSTORE

17 Gould Street
(near Yonge and Dundas)
Toronto, Ontario M5B 2K3
416-979-5116 (FAX 416-979-5175)

SPECIALTY: General books and textbooks
OWNER: Ryerson Polytechnic University
SIZE: Medium
SPECIAL SERVICES: Special orders, mail orders, book searches (online with Bowker Books in Print)
SPECIAL EVENTS: Regular sales, sidewalk sale in June and in Registration Week
GETTING THERE: Dundas subway station on Yonge line; bookstore is on the ground floor of a parking garage

The Ryerson Bookstore is a good-sized university bookstore catering to the university community. It has a section of classroom supplies, one wall of textbooks, and a substantial stock of general books in various categories including accounting, architecture, biography, biology, chemistry, children, communications, computer, cookbooks, dictionaries, engineering, environmental health, finance, French, graphic arts, history, hospitality and tourism, hotel, human resources, interior design, management, marketing, math, midwifery, nursing, philosophy, photo arts (including film), physics, politics, psychology, public administration, reference, retailing, social work, and sociology. A large sign tells students, "Please attend classes before purchasing your textbooks."

SUP BOOKSTORE

Woodside Square, Unit 127–129,
1571 Sandhurst Circle
(near Finch and McCowan)
Scarborough, Ontario M1V 1V2
416-293-2696 (FAX 416-293-9716)

SPECIALTY: Chinese literature
OWNER: Sino United Publishing Ltd.
SIZE: Medium (35,000 titles)
SPECIAL SERVICES: Special orders; regular shipments from Hong Kong
SPECIAL EVENTS: Space for rental for exhibits
GETTING THERE: Finch bus #139; McCowan bus #129; parking in mall

The SUP Bookstore, a modern, well-lighted mall bookstore, carries books in Chinese on art, astrology, business, children's books, China and Asia, computers, cookbooks, environmental studies, folk literature, health, history, hobbies (stamps, coins, decorating), language, martial arts, medical (acupuncture and massage as well as traditional approaches), modern novels, parenting, philosophy, social science, technical, textbooks for learning English, Mandarin, or Cantonese, and travel. There are also 3,000 titles in English, largely translations of Chinese literature. The store also carries CDs and cassettes of classical music.

SCIENCE CITY SCIENCE BOOK STORES

55 Bloor Street West
(Bay and Bloor, in the Concourse
Level of the Manulife Centre)
Toronto, Ontario M4W 1A1
416-968-2627 (FAX 416-968-1087)

SPECIALTY: Science books for all ages
OWNER: Dominic Riverso
SIZE: Medium
SPECIAL SERVICES: Special orders
SPECIAL EVENTS: Display of arts and crafts
GETTING THERE: Bay subway station on Bloor line; underground parking

Walk through the rainbow projected just outside the entrance and past a giant Lego giraffe and you'll find yourself in a fascinating bookstore adorned with dinosaurs, snakes, puzzles, games, toys, kites, hourglasses of all sizes, portraits of Albert Einstein, and a number of gorgeous chess sets. The book section begins with a solid general collection, arranged alphabetically by author, and continues with books arranged by subject: astronomy, biology and zoology, birds, children and child care, computer science, health and medicine, mathematics (a very large section), physics and chemistry, plants, technology, and weather. Then comes an extensive division of children's books on science, divided into aquatics, astronomy, birds, dinosaurs, games and puzzles, math, natural sciences, plants, reptiles, and a number of science books in French. This is a first-rate bookstore designed to pique and satisfy one's curiosity.

SCI-FI WORLD

1600 Steeles Avenue West
(at Dufferin)
Concord, Ontario L4K 4M2
905-738-4348 (FAX 905-737-9883)

SPECIALTY: Books, comics, gaming, memorabilia, models, toys, video games
OWNER: John J. Dimou
SIZE: Medium
SPECIAL SERVICES: Special orders, membership discounts
SPECIAL EVENTS: Author signings planned for future
GETTING THERE: Steeles bus from Finch subway station; parking in mall

Sci-Fi World describes itself as the science fiction superstore: three thousand square feet of materials under one roof. Here you will find model kits of the *U.S.S. Enterprise*, posters, collectible crystal dragons, a sizeable collection of science-fiction movies on video, rack after rack of science fiction books, including an entire bookcase of nothing but Star Trek books, books and accessories for gaming, such as Advanced Dungeons and Dragons, several Star Wars game books, and board games. The store carries a number of science fiction magazines and a large display of current and old comics. Under "S" I noted *Shazam, Secret Worlds, Spectacular Spiderman, Spelljammer, Spiderman 2099, Spooky, Star Trek, Sub-Mariner, Superman Family, Super Powers*, and *Super Villains*. Science fiction enthusiasts will want to venture north to see what owner John Dimou claims to be "Canada's largest science fiction specialty store."

SECOND TIME AROUND BOOKS

518 Mount Pleasant Road
(near Millwood)
Toronto, Ontario M4S 2M2
416-483-3227 (No FAX)

SPECIALTY: Used books, paperback and hardcover, bought and sold; old *Life* and *Rolling Stone* magazines

OWNER: Bob and Sue Lillington

SIZE: Small

SPECIAL SERVICES: Watches for particular titles for want-lists

SPECIAL EVENTS: N/A

GETTING THERE: Davisville subway station; metered parking on street

Second Time Around is a neighbourhood bookstore consisting of a single room plus the "kitchen" in the rear. The collection includes mass-market mystery, science fiction and fiction, lots of cookbooks (located, of course, in the kitchen), books for children and young adults, and travel books. In addition, there are three bookcases of trade paperbacks in fiction, philosophy, religion, women's studies, plays, poetry, and Canadiana. The old magazines find use especially for people's fiftieth wedding anniversaries and birthdays, hence the big run on issues from 1945 last year.

SEEKERS BOOKS

509 Bloor Street West, lower level
(between Bathurst and Spadina)
Toronto, Ontario M5S 1Y2
416-925-1982 (No FAX)

SPECIALTY: Spiritual and philosophical books, new and used

OWNER: Tony Merante and David Spiro

SIZE: Medium (15,000 titles)

SPECIAL SERVICES: Special orders, want lists

SPECIAL EVENTS: N/A

GETTING THERE: Bathurst or Spadina subway station; parking lots in area

Seekers Books offers books on diverse subjects, notably literature, ancient history, sociology, and archeology, but its main attraction lies in used books of a religious or philosophical nature not found in many other stores, most of them quite reasonably priced. Categories include Buddhism, comparative religions, Confucius, conspiracy and covert action, Eastern philosophy, fringe scene, Gurdjieff–Ouspensky, herbs and aromatherapy, holistic health, hypnotism, I Ching, Kabbalah, magic and alchemy, mental and psychic healing, music therapy, mysticism, Native Indians, occult studies, parapsychology, Rosicrucians, Sufism, Tai Chi, Taoism, Tarot, Yoga, and Zen. In addition, the store carries alternative CDs, principally folk and New Age music.

SHINING KNIGHT

1331 Danforth Avenue
(near Greenwood)
Toronto, Ontario M4J 1N1
416-778-8314 (No FAX)

SPECIALTY: Comic books
OWNER: Rob Carpenter
SIZE: Small
SPECIAL SERVICES: N/A
SPECIAL EVENTS: N/A
GETTING THERE: Greenwood subway station on
Bloor line; parking on street

Shining Knight is a one-room neighbourhood comic-book store offering mainline comics, a fair number of gaming books and, the most interesting feature of the store, a considerable number of large-format books. Many of these consist of collections reprinted from previously published comic books. There are also graphic novels, extended narratives portrayed in comic-book style and published as large-format trade paperbacks.

SILVER SNAIL

367 Queen Street West
(east of Spadina)
Toronto, Ontario M5V 2A4
416-593-0889 (FAX 416-593-9433)

SPECIALTY: Comics, art books, games, posters, models
OWNER: Ron Van Leeuwen
SIZE: Large
SPECIAL SERVICES: Mail orders, reserve (subscription) service
SPECIAL EVENTS: Guest appearances by writers, artists, gaming people; a modelling expert comes to the store on Saturdays
GETTING THERE: Osgoode subway station, then walk 3 blocks or take the Queen Street streetcar; parking lot across the street

The major clientele for comic-book stores seems to be males aged sixteen to thirty, a group that also participates actively in role-playing games. Silver Snail serves both interests. In addition to a large number of comics, both new and old, one finds complete paraphernalia for gaming, including organizing books, scoring books, ongoing role-playing games, and single-night adventures. Where other stores might have half a dozen books devoted to gaming, Silver Snail offers hundreds, making it the largest centre for gaming materials in the city. The store has a huge selection of back issues at competitive prices, many below the current guide prices.

SLEUTH OF BAKER STREET

1600 Bayview Avenue (south of Eglinton)
Toronto, Ontario M4G 3B7
416-483-3111 (FAX 416-483-3141)
e-mail: sleuth@inforamp.net

SPECIALTY: British, American, and Canadian crime, mystery, and espionage
OWNERS: J.D. Singh and Marian Misters
SIZE: Medium (approximately 20,000 titles in stock)
SPECIAL SERVICES: Purchases used collections of detective fiction for resale, provides a search service for book collectors, publishes a bimonthly newsletter, *Merchant of Menace*, available by subscription and in store, listing store events, author profiles, etc.
SPECIAL EVENTS: Signings, visiting authors, monthly reading club
GETTING THERE: Davisville subway station then Bayview #11 bus; metered parking on street, municipal garage at Millwood Street

Mystery lovers seeking the latest exploits of their favourite sleuth or spy novel aficionados hoping to fill in a missing volume in a series can usually find what they are looking for at Sleuth of Baker Street. A bookstore in the classic style, it has floor-to-ceiling shelves with sliding ladders to reach the extremities. In addition to hard- and softcover editions of new mystery, crime, detective, and espionage fiction, the store offers a fair-sized collection of first editions and signed copies. The staff are themselves mystery fans and will happily give advice or exchange critical opinions. Books on cassette, books for children, and books on true crime are also available.

SMITHBOOKS

Chapters Inc. Head Office
90 Ronson Drive
Toronto, Ontario M9W 1C1
416-243-3138 (FAX 416-243-8964)

SPECIALTY: General books, including best-sellers and remainders
OWNER: Chapters Inc.
SIZE: Medium
SPECIAL SERVICES: Special orders
SPECIAL EVENTS: N/A

SmithBooks offers hardcover and softcover best-sellers in fiction and non-fiction. Categories include art and photography, business and finance, Canadiana, computers, food and drink, games and puzzles, health and fitness, history and politics, home, literature, mystery, nature and science, New Age and astrology, performing arts, reference, religion and philosophy, science fiction and fantasy, sports, travel, and women's studies. The remainder tables offer coffee-table books at reduced prices. The children's sections tend to be fairly large, with books for babies and toddlers, preschool, early readers, young readers, and young adults. There are also around 500 magazines for sale. Most of the stores include several shelves of books recommended by the employees.

LOCATIONS in the greater Toronto area include: Hillcrest Mall (9350 Yonge Street, 905-423-6438); Fairview Mall (Don Mills & Sheppard, 416-499-0581); Shops at Steeles & 404 (2900 Steeles Avenue East, 905-881-1063); College Park (444 Yonge Street, 416-598-3867); Royal Bank Plaza (200 Bay Street, 416-865-0090); Queens Quay (207 Queen's Quay, 416-203-0527); Woodbine Centre (500 Rexdale Boulevard, 416-674-5690); Yorkdale Shopping Centre (3401 Dufferin Street, 416-781-6428); Yonge/Sheppard Centre (4841 Yonge Street, 416-222-1285); Yonge/Eglinton Centre (2300 Yonge Street, 416-484-9340); Toronto Dominion Centre (20 Bloor Street East, 416-969-7177); Eaton Centre (220 Yonge Street, 416-979-9376); Promenade (Promenade Circle, 905-764-0734); Queen Street East (2178 Queen Street East, 416-698-9536); Scotia Plaza (40 King Street West, 416-366-7536); Lawrence Square (700 Lawrence Avenue West, 416-782-0562); Dufferin Mall (900 Dufferin Street, 416-538-7150); and four outlets at Lester B. Pearson Airport.

SPANISH CENTRE (THE SPANISH BOOKSTORE IN TORONTO)

40 Hayden Street (near Yonge and Bloor)
Toronto, Ontario M4Y 1V8
416-515-2755 (FAX 416-515-2752)

SPECIALTY: Spanish-language books and dictionaries, books for learning Spanish, travel guides, cookbooks
OWNER: Limited corporation
SIZE: Small
SPECIAL SERVICES: Special orders, Spanish instruction
SPECIAL EVENTS: Art exhibitions, films, and conferences
GETTING THERE: Yonge and Bloor subway station; parking on street

The Spanish Centre serves both as a school and as a resource centre for those teaching and learning Spanish. There are books on learning Spanish, dictionaries, verb books, simplified stories, books for children, and general reference. In addition, the store sells Latin-American and Spanish literature at competitive prices, both in the original language and in English translation. This is one of the few bookstores in the city where one can obtain Gabriel García Márquez, Manuel Puig, Isabel Allende, Borges, Fuentes, Guiñazí, Cervantes, and Lorca in their original tongue.

SPOKEN WORD AUDIOBOOKS

350 Bay Street
(near Queen)
Toronto, Ontario M5H 2S6
416-368-1027 (FAX 416-368-0067)

SPECIALTY: Books on tape
OWNER: Graeme Cox
SIZE: Small
SPECIAL SERVICES: Rentals, mail orders, special orders from catalogue
SPECIAL EVENTS: N/A
GETTING THERE: Queen subway station on Yonge line; street or underground parking

Every book at Spoken Word Audiobooks is on tape or CD, with subjects including biography, children, classics, fiction, humour, mystery, poetry, science fiction, science and nature. The clientele consists mainly of commuters who work in the nearby business district, hence the large sections devoted to business and self-improvement. For the most part, audiotapes represent abridged versions of the original book, although there is a section of unabridged fiction. A section on radio includes programs ranging from William Shakespeare to Abbott & Costello and Sherlock Holmes. The humour section includes the works of Garrison Keillor as well as BBC productions such as the *Goon Show* and *Fawlty Towers*. In addition to the audiobooks available at the store, one can choose from a catalogue of some 59,000 titles available by special order.

SQUIBBS STATIONERS

1974 Weston Road
(north of Lawrence)
Toronto, Ontario M9N 1W2
416-241-5801 (FAX 416-241-5801)

SPECIALTY: General books, high school textbooks, Bibles, personalized stationery
OWNER: Jack and Suri Weinberg-Linshy
SIZE: Very small
SPECIAL SERVICES: Special orders on elementary and high school textbooks and ESL books
SPECIAL EVENTS: N/A
GETTING THERE: Keele subway station, #89 Weston bus north; Highway 401 to Weston Road exit, south 2 km; parking on street

Squibbs Stationers, founded in 1927, remains one of the oldest businesses in the the Weston community. Started as a commercial and social stationer, it has evolved into a bookstore carrying a full selection of high school texts, ESL texts, study guides, dictionaries, etc. Squibbs also carries children's books, Bibles, cookbooks, and a general selection of art, biographies, fiction, and historical books. In addition, the store carries stationery and a selection of unusual gift ideas. Special orders are always welcome.

SRBICA BOOKS

2238 Dundas Street West, downstairs
(south of Bloor)
Toronto, Ontario M6R 3A9
416-539-0476 (FAX 416-539-0540)
e-mail: srbica@terraport.net

SPECIALTY: Serbian books, books in English about the former Yugoslavia, Serbian language newspapers published in Belgrade and in the Diaspora
OWNER: Zivko Apic
SIZE: Small (over 3,000 titles)
SPECIAL SERVICES: Catalogues issued, special orders
SPECIAL EVENTS: Occasional lectures or poetry readings
GETTING THERE: Dundas West subway station; parking at store

Entering Srbica Books, you would never guess that you were in Toronto, for the store and its entire contents seem to have been transported from a previous era of a world that, to some extent, no longer exists. Pictures of Serbian patriots adorn the walls, and hundreds of copies of contemporary novels form a great pile in the middle of the store. On the shelves are books on literary criticism and literary biographies, the Second World War, the native guerrilla movement, Kosovo (cradle of the Serbian medieval state), Serbian history, religion, and literature, and multivolume treatises on ethnography, sociology, and the anthropology of the Balkan Peninsula. Pride of place goes to a photo-reproduction of a 13th-century manuscript and a twelve-volume history of Serbia in the 19th century. A generous number of chairs and tables form a comfortable reading area.

STEVEN TEMPLE BOOKS

489 Queen Street West, 2nd Floor
(near Spadina)
Toronto, Ontario M5V 2B4
416-865-9908 (FAX 416-865-1872)

SPECIALTY: Literary first editions, general antiquarian books, Canadian first editions in fiction, poetry, and drama
OWNER: Steven Temple
SIZE: Medium (30,000 books)
SPECIAL SERVICES: Want list searches, catalogues issued, appraisals for insurance or estate purposes
SPECIAL EVENTS: N/A
GETTING THERE: Queen Street streetcar; parking lot nearby

Steven Temple Books claims to have the world's second-largest stock of out-of-print and rare Canadian literary books. Owner Temple specializes in literary first editions, rare and antiquarian books with a focus on Canadian literature, and selected books in other areas. The store caters to collectors rather than readers, and the owner has gone to some lengths to distinguish his business from a used book store. A sign at street level, intended to discourage drop-in trade, reads, "We do not deal in dictionaries, grammars, textbooks, computers, technical, business, sociology, occult, new age, health, philosophy and religion." Temple issues catalogues to stay in touch with an international clientele, and responds promptly to orders by mail, telephone, or fax. The store is open Monday-Friday 12–6, Saturday 12–5, but the owner prefers customers to telephone first.

STORYTALE LANE

399 Roncevalles Avenue
(near Howard Park)
Toronto, Ontario M6R 2N1
416-532-1350 (FAX same)

SPECIALTY: Children's books
OWNER: Kathy Heal
SIZE: Medium
SPECIAL SERVICES: Special orders, teacher discounts, Birthday Club (a helium balloon and 15% discount)
SPECIAL EVENTS: Occasional storytelling
GETTING THERE: Dundas West subway station, #504 streetcar to Howard Park; parking on street

Storytale Lane offers a broad selection of children's books, both fiction and non-fiction. One wall is devoted to a collection of stuffed animals, while a playroom in the front has toys and a television for watching videos. Books for young readers may be found in sections marked ABC's, 123's, Time, Colours, Shapes, Opposites, and Preschool Books. Older children will find various categories to interest them: animals, Canadian storybooks, environment, fantasy, geography, history, multicultural books, mystery (Hardy Boys and Nancy Drew), plants, poems and rhymes, trees and flowers, religion, science, science fiction, sports stories, tales, myths and legends, and weather. In addition, the store has a Teachers' Corner and a section on parenting. Parents may be interested in activity books such as *Fun with Kits: Ten Exciting Designs with Easy Instructions* and *The Osborne Book of Face Painting*. Storytale Lane also sells attractive posters based on well-known children's books.

SUN WA BOOK STORE

280 Spadina Avenue
(near Dundas)
Toronto, Ontario M5T 3A5
416-977-3457 (FAX 416-596-8887)

SPECIALTY: Chinese books
OWNER: Limited company
SIZE: Medium
SPECIAL SERVICES: Accepts mail orders and special orders
SPECIAL EVENTS: N/A
GETTING THERE: Dundas Street streetcar; underground parking in mall

The Sun Wa Book Store, largest of the Chinese bookstores in the central downtown area, presents its collection in tightly arranged stacks in the style of a library. The store sells a variety of dictionaries both textual and pictorial (Chinese/English, Vietnamese/English, children's Chinese/Chinese, dictionary of traditional Chinese medicine) as well as books in many fields: biographies of European and Chinese figures, business, calligraphy, Chinese translations of English literature, Chinese history in story form, classical poetry, classical literature, contemporary novels, cookbooks, design, erotic literature, family and child care, gambling, health, legendary novels, mathematics and science, novelizations of movies (including *Forrest Gump*!), parapsychology (fortune-telling), photography, politics of China and Taiwan, psychology, religion, science fiction, and self-improvement. The store also sells magazines, books on Mandarin and Cantonese, and videos for learning English and popular Hong Kong TV soap operas.

SURPRISE COMPANY

1232A Bloor Street West, lower level
(near Lansdowne)
Toronto, Ontario M6H 1N3
416-533-6009 or 1-800-668-1480
(FAX 416-533-1773)

SPECIALTY: Ethiopian and East African literature
OWNER: Fasil Kasa
SIZE: Very small
SPECIAL SERVICES: Résumé, fax, income tax
SPECIAL EVENTS: N/A
GETTING THERE: Lansdowne subway station; parking on street

The Surprise Company serves the Ethiopian community as importer, exporter, distributor, and manufacturer of artwork, books, magazines, newspapers, posters, postcards, tapes, and videos. In addition, it provides résumé, income tax, and fax services. The book collection includes literature and children's books in Ethiopian and several dialects: Amharic, Tigrina, Arabic, and Guragué. There are newspapers and magazines in Amharic and English including the *Ethiopian Review*, the *Ethiopian Register*, and *Time* magazine edited for Ethiopia. The cassettes on sale represent all the ethnic groups of Ethiopia.

SWEDENBORG BOOK CENTRE

279 Burnhamthorpe Road (near
Kipling, enter at Olivet Church)
Etobicoke, Ontario M9B 1Z6
416-233-3929 (FAX 416-239-4935)

SPECIALTY: The works of Emanuel Swedenborg,
life after death, the human mind, a rational
approach to the Bible, and related topics
OWNER: Olivet Church; manager of the book
centre, John Parker
SIZE: Small
SPECIAL SERVICES: Mail orders
SPECIAL EVENTS: N/A
GETTING THERE: Burnhamthorpe Road bus from
Islington subway station; parking on premises

The Swedenborg Book centre is devoted exclusively to
books by, about, or related to the Swedish theologian,
philosopher, and scientist Emanuel Swedenborg (1688–
1772). Swedenborg mastered Hebrew, Greek, Latin,
German, French, Italian, English, Dutch, and Swedish,
and is said to have possessed most of human knowledge
available in his time. At Olivet Church, in which the
bookstore itself is located, worship focuses on Swedenborg's teachings. A devout Christian as well as a scientist, Swedenborg explored the human anatomy in an
attempt to locate the soul. Swedenborg wrote in Latin
in order to have a language not subject to change.
Available is a newsletter published by Information
Swedenborg, distributed all across Canada.

SWIPE BOOKS ON DESIGN

234 Bay Street
(near King)
Toronto, Ontario M5K 1B2
416-363-1332 (FAX 416-363-6130)

SPECIALTY: Commercial art, graphic design,
illustration, photography, interior design,
industrial design, landscape
OWNER: Incorporated; Tina Hadjidimitriou,
president
SIZE: Small
SPECIAL SERVICES: Special orders, mail orders
SPECIAL EVENTS: Occasional designer samples,
expositions, book launches
GETTING THERE: King subway station on Yonge
line; parking lots in vicinity

Swipe Books on Design, which also goes by the name
Indx: The Design Exchange Store, occupies one corner of the Design Exchange, located in the former
Toronto Stock Exchange Building. Serving as a
resource centre for professional designers, the store
offers books on advertising, architecture, commercial
interiors, copyright-free designs (published by Dover
Books), corporate identity, fashion, graphic design,
illustration, industrial design, landscape architecture
and urban planning, marketing, multimedia, packag-
ing, typography, and writing/copywriting, as well as
innovative new products and gifts produced by the
Exchange. The Design Exchange describes itself as "a
non-profit centre for design and innovation" whose
goal is "to promote design as a tool for economic
growth and international competitiveness." In addition to the bookstore, the Design Exchange offers
exhibitions, presentations, seminars and workshops,
and operates a small cafe.

TEN EDITIONS BOOKSTORE

698 Spadina Avenue (near Bloor)
Toronto, Ontario M5S 2J2
416-964-3803 (No FAX)

SPECIALTY: Out-of-print books bought and sold, including Canadiana, children's books and ephemera, and general antiquarian books
OWNER: Susan Duff
SIZE: Large
SPECIAL SERVICES: N/A
SPECIAL EVENTS: N/A
GETTING THERE: Spadina subway station; parking next door

Ten Editions contains an amazing number of books in a relatively small space, with floor-to-ceiling bookcases running eleven shelves high, more shelves in the middle of the floor, and several back rooms crammed with books. Here one finds out-of-print books in a variety of categories: advertisement, American history, Ancient Greece and Rome, architecture, Arctic and Antarctica, Canadian biography, literature and history, clocks, dictionaries, fables, fairy tales, fashion, folklore, furniture, ghost stories, heraldry, literature (one entire wall), local histories of Toronto and Ontario, military, music, mystery, natural history, naval, organized crime, plays, police, religion, Russian history, sports, theatre, toys, stamps, UFOs, and World War II. Where does the name come from? The owner's mother had ten children!

THEATREBOOKS

11 St. Thomas Street
(near Bay and Bloor)
Toronto, Ontario M5S 2B7
416-922-7175 (FAX 416-922-0739)

SPECIALTY: Books on the performing arts, film, opera, theatre, dance, media studies
OWNERS: Leonard McHardy and John Harvey
SIZE: Medium
SPECIAL SERVICES: Special orders and mail orders
SPECIAL EVENTS: Readings, performances, workshops
GETTING THERE: Bay or Museum subway station; limited parking adjacent to store

Theatrebooks, a perennial favourite of the arts community, has re-established itself in beautiful quarters in two floors of a spacious brick building. Theatrebooks carries titles on plays, acting, dance, music, opera, and theatre, as might be found in a large general bookstore, but also offers more specialized books on film studies, screenplays, film biographies, and media studies. There are technical books on theatre and film covering such areas as cinematography, film scoring, lighting design, special effects, stage lighting, stage management, stock scenery construction, television production, and make-up for theatre, film, and television. Here one will find a dozen volumes of *Acting with an Accent*, each with cassette, *The Dictionary of Film Quotations*, and *The Monologue Index: A Guide to 1778 Monologues from 1074 Plays*. Theatrebooks carries more than fifty magazines and journals, and issues annotated catalogues in various areas.

THIRD WORLD BOOKS & CRAFTS, INC.

942 Bathurst Street (near Bloor)
Toronto, Ontario M5R 3G5
416-537-8039 (FAX 416-537-9783)

SPECIALTY: African, Caribbean, Latin American, and Asian books and crafts
OWNER: Leonard and Gwendolyn Johnson
SIZE: Medium (10,000 titles)
SPECIAL SERVICES: Special orders
SPECIAL EVENTS: Occasional book launches and poetry readings
GETTING THERE: Bathurst subway station; metered parking on street

Third World Books & Crafts is more than just a bookstore: it's a veritable celebration of Black culture worldwide. The rich decor seems to convey an almost rhythmic quality, the walls alive with pictures, paintings of political leaders, artifacts, and dolls. The children's corner includes books, a table, chairs, and a drum! The friendly reception offered by the owners contributes to the warm atmosphere of the store. The categories of books include Africa, America, art, Black American, Black novelists, Blacks in Canada, Caribbean, cookbooks, health, history, Latin America, literature, political studies, and religions. The store also carries a variety of videos and cassettes as well as magazines on Black culture.

THIS AIN'T THE ROSEDALE LIBRARY

483 Church Street (near Wellesley)
Toronto, Ontario M4Y 2C6
416-929-9912 (No FAX)

SPECIALTY: New fiction, gay and lesbian fiction and non-fiction, baseball
OWNER: Charlie Huisken and Dan Bazuin
SIZE: Small
SPECIAL SERVICES: Special orders
SPECIAL EVENTS: "Read 'em and meet 'em" — spotlight on local writers; postcards depicting visits by authors
GETTING THERE: Wellesley subway station; parking on street

This Ain't the Rosedale Library occupies a long, narrow space with walls lined with books mostly facing outward so that you get lots of visual impressions. Unfamiliar visual impressions, one might add, since the store offers many books not found elsewhere. The collection is separated into AIDS/HIV and health, cookbooks, essays, fiction (mostly trade paperbacks), film and music, gender studies, native studies, nature, psychology, and self-help, with a separate room for children's books and a considerable collection of books on baseball. A relatively large proportion of the stock consists of high-quality remainders and books at discount, so that the browser can be assured of finding not only interesting reading but bargains as well.

TIDDELY POM
BOOKS FOR CHILDREN

47A Colborne Street
(near King and Church)
Toronto, Ontario M5E 1E3
416-366-0290 (No FAX)

SPECIALTY: Children's books, some tapes and videos
OWNER: Stauffer Smith and Elizabeth Vernon
SIZE: Medium
SPECIAL SERVICES: Special orders, mail orders
SPECIAL EVENTS: N/A
GETTING THERE: King subway station, Miranda Street exit; parking lot at Market Square

How do you amuse kids in strollers while you're looking at books? Provide lots of attractive book posters, mounted on hanging divider curtains all about the store. On a recent visit, the main window contained a toy soldier amid representations of Maurice Sendak's "Wild Things," flanked by rainbow-striped pillars and pictures of Winnie the Pooh on the outside wall. Inside, one finds books for children young and old, including hardbound classics such as *Robin Hood* and *Treasure Island* as well as such perennial series as the Hardy Boys, Nancy Drew, and the works of C.S. Lewis and Dr. Seuss.

TOP BANANA

639 Mt. Pleasant Avenue
(between Davisville and Eglinton)
Toronto, Ontario M4S 2M9
416-440-0111 (FAX 416-441-8815)

SPECIALTY: Children's books
OWNER: Nancy Green and Brenda Bickram
SIZE: Small (around 4,000 titles)
SPECIAL SERVICES: N/A
SPECIAL EVENTS: Occasional Saturday visits from costumed book characters such as Franklin the Turtle, Madeline, and Clifford
GETTING THERE: Eglinton subway station; parking on street before 4 p.m.

Top Banana belongs to a group of small bookstores situated along the stretch of Mt. Pleasant Avenue south of Eglinton that includes an attractive park with wading pool. The book collection occupies a series of alcoves associated with the toys and crafts that form the major portion of the store's business. Here one finds game books, craft books, board books, lots of touch 'n' listen books, and a revolving display devoted to the works of Robert Munsch. Reading corners equipped with small chairs and beanbag chairs provide an inviting atmosphere for young browsers while the arrangement of books on the shelves, front-facing and overlapping, gives easy access and a bit of a view of the covers.

TORONTO CHRISTIAN BOOK CENTRE

651 Mount Pleasant Avenue
(south of Eglinton)
Toronto, Ontario M4S 2N2
416-481-4868 (No FAX)

SPECIALTY: Books on religion, including Bibles, Bible commentaries, children's books, records, cassettes, compact discs
OWNER: John Whitley
SIZE: Medium (around 10,000 titles)
SPECIAL SERVICES: Mail orders, special orders within one week
SPECIAL EVENTS: N/A
GETTING THERE: Bus from St. Clair or Eglinton subway station; parking on street

The collection at the Toronto Christian Book Centre comprises two overlapping divisions. On one hand, there are books for students and professionals in the field of religion, such as Bibles and Bible commentaries, archaeology, Christian apologetics, counselling, doctrinal topics, language studies, pastoral studies, prayer, and theology. On the other hand, there are books devoted to Christian living for lay people, including books on Christian marriage, cults, death and dying, devotional reading, New Age movements, women's studies, works of C.S. Lewis, a gray category called Christian fiction, and a separate room of children's books. The store sells a number of videos and has access to thousands more.

TORONTO COMPUTER BOOKS, INC.

521 Yonge Street (near Maitland)
Toronto, Ontario M4Y 1Y4
416-925-2088 (FAX 416-925-3471)
e-mail: tcb@io.org

SPECIALTY: Computer books: technical manuals, computer magazines, artificial intelligence, fuzzy logic
OWNER: Agnes Szeto
SIZE: Medium
SPECIAL SERVICES: Special orders
SPECIAL EVENTS: N/A
GETTING THERE: Wellesley subway station; public parking nearby

Form follows function at Toronto Computer Books, where white slotted walls allow shelves to be placed virtually anywhere. Atop the bookshelves lie old computers, vestiges of an earlier policy of trading customers books for obsolete computers. The store attempts to stock most computer books in print and will soon be carrying CD-ROM products as well. The current categories include accounting, assembly language, C, C++, databases, DOS, games, general, graphics, hardware, languages, Macintosh, multimedia, OS/2, spreadsheets, theory, Windows, and word processing. It is difficult to imagine a topic in computer science for which Toronto Computer Books cannot offer a resource.

TORONTO WOMEN'S BOOK STORE

73 Harbord Street (near Spadina)
Toronto, Ontario M5S 1G4
416-922-8744 (FAX 416-922-1417)

SPECIALTY: Books by and about women: fiction with a feminist slant, psychology, violence, lesbianism
OWNER: Non-profit company
SIZE: Small (5,000 titles)
SPECIAL SERVICES: Mail orders, special orders, referral service (to counselors or for health information)
SPECIAL EVENTS: Readings, workshops, group meetings
GETTING THERE: Spadina subway station; parking on street

The Toronto Women's Book Store welcomes customers with a modern, airy display area brightened by skylights and flowers. A well-organized bulletin board presents information on networking, classes, workshops, and calls for submission of poetry and papers. The collection provides an excellent resource for students and researchers in women's studies as well as a variety of books of interest to the general reader. There is a large collection of lesbian fiction and non-fiction as well as books on special issues, such as ethnofeminism, ethnic groups, and women in developing countries. The store carries a wide assortment of feminist magazines and includes a small children's section.

TOWER RECORDS

2 Queen Street West
(at Yonge)
Toronto, Ontario M5H 3X4
416-593-2500 (FAX 416-593-7995)

SPECIALTY: Books about music, alternative literature (underground writings), pop culture, sex, drugs, body art, murder, mayhem, computers, small press magazines
OWNER: Tower Records
SIZE: Medium
SPECIAL SERVICES: Special orders on stock in database
SPECIAL EVENTS: Monthly reading nights
GETTING THERE: Queen subway station on Yonge line; parking garages in area

Tower Records, endorsing cross-promotion of products, distributes its books into three different collections, each representing and taking on the character of the tapes and CDs also sold in that division. On the second floor, one finds a quiet alcove containing a fine selection of books on classical music, including four books on or about John Cage and recent scholarly studies on Mozart, Beethoven, Mahler, and Debussy, as well as books on opera, music dictionaries, and more than thirty music journals (one in German). On the third floor, one wall is lined with a good collection of books on jazz, pop, and blues, with biographies as well as studies of the music itself. In the basement, one encounters a loud, in-your-face atmosphere featuring books on sex, drugs, body art, murder, film, and alternative literature, as well as a magazine section containing hundreds of titles divided into adult, cars, computers, music, and New Age. Both the book and magazine sections on this floor include small press materials not to be found in most general bookstores.

THE TOY CIRCUS

2036 Queen Street East
(near Lee Avenue)
Toronto, Ontario M4L 1J4
416-699-4971 (No fax)

SPECIALTY: Children's books
OWNER: Donald and Betty Graham
SIZE: Small
SPECIAL SERVICES: Special orders
SPECIAL EVENTS: N/A
GETTING THERE: Queen Street streetcar; parking
  on street

The Toy Circus offers a small book collection in the context of a general toy store. The books range from board books to the Berenstain Bears, with classic novels (*Eloise* is back in print!), fairy tales, counting books, dictionaries, Canadiana, and a few books in French. Parents will find helpful instruction books on making braids and bows, bracelets, or knight's helmets. The Toy Circus has the complete offerings of certain publishers, notably the Ladybird Books (Read It Yourself) and books published by Annick Press. A plaque lists the winners in the Beaches Spring Sprint for runners six years old and under, sponsored by the Toy Circus.

THE TOY SHOP

62 Cumberland Street
(near Bay and Bloor)
Toronto, Ontario M4W 1J5
416-961-4870 (FAX 416-961-4892)

SPECIALTY: Children's books
OWNER: Don and Betty Graham
SIZE: Very small
SPECIAL SERVICES: Special orders
SPECIAL EVENTS: N/A
GETTING THERE: Bloor/Yonge subway station;
  municipal parking adjacent

The Top Shop, though primarily a high-end toy store, also has a small section devoted to books, ranging from board books to young adult. Many books are displayed facing out, with concealed lighting producing a happy effect. Categories include beginning readers, Canadian authors, classics, crafts, dictionaries, fairy tales, French books, picture books, science, and an interesting section of poetry classics illustrated for children, including works of Robert Frost and Edgar Allan Poe. The Toy Shop also carries a variety of tapes and videos. The collection, though small, reflects a discriminating taste.

TREASURE ISLAND TOYS

311 Danforth Avenue
(near Chester)
Toronto, Ontario M4K 1N7
416-778-4913 (FAX 416-778-0083)

SPECIALTY: Children's books
OWNER: Ingrid Mukans and Lilian Starastas
SIZE: Small
SPECIAL SERVICES: Special orders and loot bags
SPECIAL EVENTS: Face-painting on Hallowe'en
GETTING THERE: Chester subway station on Bloor line; parking on street

The books at Treasure Island Toys are surrounded by stuffed animals, toys, and crafts. The store carries the Stoddart Eyewitness series of science books, a nice selection of books from Annick Press, the School Zone educational books, Spider puzzle books, young teen romances, and craft books amid models, craft supplies, puppets, and dolls.

TRILLIUM BOOKS

120 Adelaide Street, concourse level
(near York and Adelaide)
Toronto, Ontario M5H 1T1
416-367-9245 (No FAX)

SPECIALTY: General, mainly business, children, cookbooks, health, and magazines
OWNER: Elaine Albrektsen
SIZE: Medium
SPECIAL SERVICES: Special orders, mail orders
SPECIAL EVENTS: Occasional author signings
GETTING THERE: Osgoode subway station; parking under City Hall

Trillium Books is a small, general bookstore offering books on business, Canadiana, cookbooks, crafts, do-it-yourself, fiction, fine arts, games, gardening, health, history, humour, literature, music, mystery, nature, New Age, occult, philosophy, photography, psychology, reference, religion, science fiction, science, sports, and travel. The store includes a nice section of recent fiction in trade paperback as well as reprints of books published in the 1920s and 1930s such as *Tidal Swings of the Stock Market*.

TRISKELION

1081 Bathurst Street
(just south of Dupont)
Toronto, Ontario M5R 3G8
416-588-3727 (FAX 416-782-4598)

SPECIALTY: Used books, and some new, in a variety of areas, with a concentration in spiritual books, especially Celtic

OWNER: John and Stephanie Boyle, Pierre de Margerie

SIZE: Medium (around 15,000 volumes)

SPECIAL SERVICES: Book searches, mail orders

SPECIAL EVENTS: Classes and speakers on meditation and personal development; group meetings on radionics and psychic development

GETTING THERE: Bathurst subway station, then south one-half block; metered parking on street

Triskelion, one of Toronto's newest bookstores, has as its motto *Corff, enaid ac yspryd*, Welsh for body, mind and spirit. The name is a Greek symbol for a three-legged man, the number three being intertwined with one and two to represent an eternal unity without end. The owners buy and sell books in certain areas, notably art, history, literature, music, and spirituality. (For the casual browser, there are also sections of paperbacks in science fiction and mysteries.) The store manages to display an enormous number of books in a small space, with bookcases rising twelve shelves high (a number of ladders provide access to the upper extremes). The owners are still establishing the direction the store will take, but it already provides a centre for classes, lectures, and group meetings on various areas of spirituality.

TROYKA LIMITED

799 College Street
(at Ossington)
Toronto, Ontario M6C 1C7
416-535-6693 (FAX 416-535-3265)

SPECIALTY: Russian language books and Russian crafts

OWNER: Russian Federation

SIZE: Small

SPECIAL SERVICES: N/A

SPECIAL EVENTS: N/A

GETTING THERE: College Street streetcar; parking on street

Troyka Limited purveys imported tea, chocolate, porcelain figures, jewelry, all sizes of nesting dolls, videos, and books to the city's Russian community. The book collection, which occupies a full wall of the store, includes best-sellers, children's books, classic literature, dictionaries, encyclopedias, health, maps, modern literature poetry, religion, textbooks for adults and children to learn English or Russian, and travel. The store also carries several dozen Russian-language newspapers, albums of art, and sale books.

UKRAINIAN BOOKS AND GIFT STORE

2282 Bloor Street West
(near Runnymede)
Toronto, Ontario M6S 1N9
416-762-8651 (FAX 416-767-6839)

SPECIALTY: Books in Ukrainian and
  English-language translations
OWNER: Family-owned business
SIZE: Very small (fewer than 1,000 titles)
SPECIAL SERVICES: Mail orders, discounts to
  schools on textbooks
SPECIAL EVENTS: N/A
GETTING THERE: Runnymede subway station;
  municipal parking lot nearby

The Ukrainian Books and Gift Store delights the eye with unusual sights such as an entire section of Ukrainian Easter eggs and another of Ukrainian embroidery. The small book collection contains a large proportion of children's books, some in English and Ukrainian, such as *Sonja's First Camp* and *I Want to Dance*. All the books face up on flat shelves, so one's eye is caught by the illustrated covers of books such as *The Lost Architecture of Kiev*, *Wooden Churches in the Carpathians*, *The Ukrainian Impact on Russian Culture 1750–1850*, *Ukraine during World War II: History and Its Aftermath* and *A History of Ukrainian Settlement in Canada*. The store also carries Russian-language newspapers, a large number of cassettes, and sheet music, including vocal music for children, and Ukrainian folk songs arranged for piano duet.

ULYSSES TRAVEL BOOKSHOP

101 Yorkville Avenue (near Avenue Road)
Toronto, Ontario M5R 1C1
416-323-3609 or 1-800-268-4395
(FAX 416-323-3609)
e-mail: 76202.3074@compuserve.com

SPECIALTY: Travel books and maps, travel guides
OWNER: Marcia Green
SIZE: Small
SPECIAL SERVICES: Mail orders, special orders to
  anywhere in the world
SPECIAL EVENTS: Occasional author signings
GETTING THERE: Bay subway station; private
  parking lots in the area

Ulysses Travel Bookshop endeavours to meet a variety of travel needs. There are guides to cities, countries, and regions, guides to bed-and-breakfast accommodations, guides for walking tours and boating excursions, books on Canadian national parks, vacation suggestions for travellers with disabilities, foreign language dictionaries, phrase books and cassettes, and a complete set of Michelin guides. One can also find travel paraphernalia such as road atlases, tips for packing, children's travel game books, and maps ranging from city maps and road maps to historical reprint maps (depicting, for example, the Battle of Normandy) and an enormous twelve-piece world map.

THE BOOK ROOM

More than you'd think...

Come and visit us for a wide selection of resources. Topics such as: *addiction, aging, counseling issues, health and healing, social concerns, spirituality, meditations, children's books and children's concerns, wedding supplies, gifts and merchandise,* and much much more!

MANY SPECIAL SERVICES

- We provide consultation for libraries, study groups, and can provide special evening events for groups!

- We have developed special lists that highlight the best books for a variety of subjects!

- If you are looking for a book and are unable to find it in our store – Don't worry – we'll get it for you. We specialize in special orders!

Come and visit us today!

We are located on the subway line at Islington subway, we have free underground parking, free coffee, comfy chairs in front of sunny windows and the friendliest & most helpful staff in town!

For store hours and more information on our special events please call us at (416) 231-6597 or fax at (416) 232-6001

THE UNITED CHURCH BOOK ROOM

3250 Bloor Street West
Etobicoke, ON M8X 2Y4

UNITED CHURCH BOOK ROOM

3250 Bloor Street West
(at Islington)
Etobicoke, Ontario M8X 2Y4
416-231-6597 (FAX 416-232-6001)

SPECIALTY: Religious books, psychology, devotions, spirituality, theology, church, family, personal growth
OWNER: United Church of Canada
SIZE: Medium
SPECIAL SERVICES: Mail orders, telephone orders
SPECIAL EVENTS: occasional author signings
GETTING THERE: Islington subway station on Bloor line; parking on street or free underground parking

The United Church Book Room in its new quarters occupies a bright, airy space, with one entire wall in glass and light-wood panelling throughout. The collection, neatly displayed in well-labelled, shoulder-height shelves, includes addiction, aging, Bible study, Bibles, biography, children and spirituality, children in crisis, children and the environment, children's fiction, Christian education, church development, church school resources, commentaries, counselling issues, devotions, fiction, games, grief, health and healing, men's issues, music, Old Testament, pastoral care, personal growth, pluralism, sale books, sermon resources, social concerns, spirituality, staff recommendations, study resources, support group study, teens, theology, women's issues, worship resources, and youth study. Soft sacred music in the background, comfortable sitting areas (with small chairs in the children's reading area), and a friendly, helpful staff make browsing a pleasure.

UNITEXT

Mayfair Plaza,
4699 Keele Street
(at Steeles)
Toronto, Ontario M3J 2N8
416-665-9510 (FAX 416-665-9516)

SPECIALTY: Textbooks for York University
OWNER: Cohen and Spiegel
SIZE: Medium
SPECIAL SERVICES: Special orders
SPECIAL EVENTS: N/A
GETTING THERE: Steeles #60C and #106 buses; parking in front of store

Unitext, formerly University Textbook Supply, serves as an adjunct to York University both in location and in function. In a procedure resembling that of Consumers Distributing, students look up their courses in a catalogue, fill out a slip, and hand it to a clerk, who picks out the required texts from a veritable book warehouse with shelves twenty feet high. Books are available either new or used, and the store will buy back textbooks when students are finished with them. A second branch of the store, serving as an adjunct to University of Toronto, may be found at 243 College Street, at Spadina (416-977-0710).

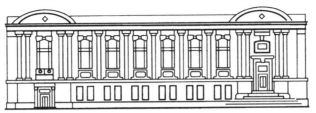

After you've bought your

computer, athletic gear,

stationery and office supplies,

textbooks, magazines and professional

journals and periodicals, sale books,

postage stamps and courier services,

custom published course packages,

tickets to our latest author reading,

let's discuss the real reason you

want to spend hours browsing here—

thousands, upon thousands of

books situated in Toronto's

former central reference library.

general interest • academic • computer
• scientific & technical • medical

UNIVERSITY OF TORONTO BOOKSTORE

214 College Street (at St. George)
Toronto, Ontario M5T 3A1
416-978-7900 (FAX 416-978-7242)

SPECIALTY: General and academic
OWNER: University of Toronto Press Inc.; Ron Johnson, manager
SIZE: Large (75,000 titles in trade books, 10,000 medical) — Canada's largest textbook store (new & used)
SPECIAL SERVICES: Special orders, Canada-wide shipping, custom publishing packages for professors, computer shop
SPECIAL EVENTS: *University of Toronto Bookstore Review*, three times a year; an on-going series of events, including lectures and readings of poetry and fiction
GETTING THERE: Queen's Park subway station or College Street streetcar; parking on street before 4 p.m.

Plan to spend a good deal of time when you visit the University of Toronto Bookstore. The vast collection occupies a handsome high-ceilinged hall divided by wooden bookcases into nook-like arrangements that encourage browsing. Trade books, located in the great hall, are divided into some eighty classifications, from Africa to Writing and Style. There are many display tables featuring new books, remainders, autographed books, and books published by the University of Toronto Press. Textbooks occupy a separate level. Much smaller collections, consisting primarily of textbooks, may be found at the Erindale, Scarborough, and Victoria University campuses. A new location at Victoria University carries new and used textbooks and a wide variety of trade titles. All locations buy back textbooks from customers.

USED BOOKS, ETC.

22 Balliol Mews
(near Yonge and Davisville)
Toronto, Ontario M5S 1C1
416-489-5170 (No FAX)

SPECIALTY: Used books
OWNER: Patricia Lillie
SIZE: Small
SPECIAL SERVICES: Owner will watch for particular books
SPECIAL EVENTS: N/A
GETTING THERE: Davisville subway station on Yonge line; parking in plaza

What's in a name? As the only establishment listed in the white pages of the telephone book under "used books," this bookstore gets business from travellers passing through the city in addition to the usual clientele of a neighbourhood used book store. Located above the Lazy Lizard Grill and Bar, the store features a lifelike model reclining on a wicker bench reading a Len Deighton novel. One finds paperback books in the usual categories as well as a number of hardcover books at reasonable prices (e.g., E.L. Doctorow's *Billy Bathgate* sells for $5). Owner Patricia Lillie calls attention to the store's pine bookshelves and reminds customers that there is no tax on used books.

VIET NAM BOOKSTORE

415 Spadina Avenue (near College)
Toronto, Ontario M5T 2G6
416-595-5199 (FAX same)

SPECIALTY: Books in Vietnamese, a few English translations
OWNER: Eddie Tran
SIZE: Small
SPECIAL SERVICES: Special orders, mail orders worldwide
SPECIAL EVENTS: N/A
GETTING THERE: Spadina bus or College streetcar; metered parking on street

The Viet Nam Bookstore, a small room decorated with Chinese movie posters on the wall, serves the local Vietnamese community, as well as the Toronto Public Library, with a variety of books in Vietnamese including French-Vietnamese dictionaries, English-Vietnamese dictionaries, and a number of specialized dictionaries including an English-Vietnamese-Chinese computer dictionary. Other categories include children's books, computers, history, literature, mathematics, medical, music, novels, poetry, politics, religion (based on either the Bible or Buddhist texts), and travel. The store also sells videos and compact discs of Vietnamese music.

VILLAGE BOOK STORE

239 Queen Street West
(near University)
Toronto, Ontario M5V 1Z4
416-598-4097 (No FAX)

SPECIALTY: New and used books on Canadiana, decorative arts, collectibles, antiques
OWNER: Eric Wellington and Nancy Kwak
SIZE: Medium (50,000 titles)
SPECIAL SERVICES: Want-list for clients, searches in certain areas, mail orders, special orders in their fields
SPECIAL EVENTS: Annual half-price sale
GETTING THERE: Osgoode subway station; parking on street

The Village Book Store carries new and used books in a number of areas. Well-known in Canada, the store receives frequent referrals from other bookstores in its specialities, which include art, art criticism, art history, art reference, artist biographies, books about books, Canadian fiction, Canadian history, Canadian art, design, fiction, literary criticism, literary biography, and out-of-print antique books. The store has a sizeable antiquarian collection including everything from music to cookbooks. In addition, one finds a large general history section, a section of children's books, some musical scores, and a file of film photos.

VILLAGE LIBRARY AND BOOK SHOP

437 Spadina Road
(near Lonsdale)
Toronto, Ontario M5P 2W3
416-483-4563 (FAX 416-932-0853)

SPECIALTY: Best-sellers
OWNER: Tom Partridge
SIZE: Small
SPECIAL SERVICES: Recommendations to readers
SPECIAL EVENTS: N/A
GETTING THERE: St. Clair streetcar to Spadina; nearby municipal parking lot

The Village Library occupies a niche between the gift shop at the front of the narrow store and a post office substation in the rear. Here, readers may purchase the latest John Grisham or Danielle Steel novels, or other books such as *The Kennedy Women: The Saga of an American Family* or *The Kids Cottage Book*. For a neighbourhood bookstore, the Village Library offers a considerable number of books for children and teens, including children's classics, both hardbound and paperback, and racks of Nancy Drew, the Hardy Boys, Fear Street, and Beverly Hills 90210. Cookbooks, gift books, paperback mysteries and adventure stories, and a selection of 400 magazines complete the collection, in a store that has been serving this neighbourhood since 1930.

VINCE ODDY BRIDGE BOOKS, GAMES AND SUPPLIES

27 Barrymore Road
(near McCowan and Lawrence)
Toronto, Ontario M1J 1W1
416-289-1434 or 1-800-463-9815 (No FAX)

SPECIALTY: Bridge books
OWNER: Vince Oddy
SIZE: Very small
SPECIAL SERVICES: Mail orders; special orders for any bridge book in print
SPECIAL EVENTS: N/A
GETTING THERE: McCowan Road bus from Warden subway station; parking on street

Of all the specialized bookstores in Toronto, Vince Oddy's occupies probably the narrowest niche of all. The store carries 300 titles on bridge, ranging from general books such as *Commonsense Bidding* and *Why You Lose at Bridge*, to specialized pamphlets such as *Minor Suit Raises* and *One Notrump Forcing*. There is also bridge-related software, card tables and chairs, as well as boards for duplicate bridge, playing cards, and other club supplies. The entire collection is set up, appropriately enough, on card tables.

VOLUMES VOLUMES VOLUMES

74 Front Street East
(between Church and Jarvis)
Toronto, Ontario M5E 1T7
416-366-9522 (No FAX)

SPECIALTY: General fiction, strongest in
  20th-century literature and children's books
OWNER: Philip Dodd, manager
SIZE: Very small
SPECIAL SERVICES: Special orders, gift-wrapping,
  books on hold
SPECIAL EVENTS: Art gallery rotated on a monthly
  basis, occasional book launches
GETTING THERE: King subway station; nearby
  underground parking

Fluorescent ceiling lights on pale walls and carpet produce a somewhat sterile atmosphere, while standing metal bookshelves convey an impression of impermanence in this relatively new bookstore. For all that, Volumes Volumes Volumes is a neighbourhood bookstore with a worthy collection of children's books, a selection of 20th-century literature, and a substantial number of trade paperbacks. Categories include business, Canadiana, cookbooks, crafts, fantasy/science fiction, fiction, games, gardening, mystery, New Age, philosophy, psychology, reference, remainders, and women's issues. The store also carries around 600 magazines.

WATKINS BOOK EXCHANGE

2996 Danforth Avenue
(near Victoria Park)
Toronto, Ontario M4C 1M7
Unlisted telephone; no FAX

SPECIALTY: Book exchange
OWNER: Margaret Watkins
SIZE: Very small
SPECIAL SERVICES: N/A
SPECIAL EVENTS: N/A
GETTING THERE: Victoria Park subway station;
  parking on street

The Watkins Book Exchange began over fifty years ago as a convenience store and book exchange. Gradually it added penny candy, potatoes, cigarettes, and groceries, at a time when Danforth and Victoria Park stood a fair distance from the city proper. There used to be a large stock of books in storage; now everything is on display, including classics, history books, mysteries, novels, romances, science fiction, and war stories, nearly all mass-market paperbacks. There are a few hardbound books and some extraordinary bargains to be had (for example, John Updike's *Couples* in hardback for $2). Mounted on the wall is a newspaper article written about the store in its glory days.

WEST ARKA

2282 Bloor Street West
(near Runnymede)
Toronto, Ontario M6S 1N9
416-762-8751 (FAX 4416-767-6839)

SPECIALTY: Ukrainian books and gifts
OWNER: West Arka Company
SIZE: Small
SPECIAL SERVICES: N/A
SPECIAL EVENTS: N/A
GETTING THERE: Runnymede subway station on Bloor line; parking on street

West Arka's book section, which occupies the back of a gift shop, contains a little bit of everything: art (with a number of books on Ukrainian Easter eggs), Bibles and Bible stories, books on embroidery, catechisms for children, children's storybooks, books on conversational Ukrainian, cookbooks, dictionaries and educational materials, encyclopedias, English translations of Ukrainian literature, history (with a good many in English, including two books on Chernobyl), prayerbooks, and Ukrainian grammar books for beginners. One also finds a dozen Ukrainian-language newspapers and a dozen magazines and quarterly journals.

WHAT THE DICKENS BOOKSTORE CAFE

66 Gerrard Street East (at Church)
Toronto, Ontario M50 1P3
416-599-8211 (FAX 416-977-7993)

SPECIALTY: Used books on design, art, literature, and other subjects
OWNER: Randy Urquhart and Maureen Kahn
SIZE: Medium
SPECIAL SERVICES: Informal searches and requests, coffee, muffins
SPECIAL EVENTS: N/A
GETTING THERE: Carlton streetcar to Church, walk south three blocks; parking on street

Hidden away down a short hallway and through a beautiful brick archway lies a space that has served in the past as a CBC rehearsal studio, a bar, a pool hall and, in an earlier reincarnation as now, a bookstore. The largest category comprises books on movies and drama, which seem to run throughout the store. Other subjects, somewhat erratically labelled, include American and European history, architecture, art, biography, Canadian history, food and wine, literature, plays, psychiatry, reference and science, as well as a good section of hardcover mysteries. As with many used book stores, the stock has outpaced the available space, resulting in a manageable mess. Browsers can purchase coffee, juices, muffins, or desserts and then sit at one of half a dozen tables to peruse their selections.

WIND IN THE WILLOWS

403 Jane Street (at Annette,
midway between Bloor and Dundas)
Toronto, Ontario M6S 3Z6
416-769-4518 (NO FAX)

SPECIALTY: Children's books (within a store selling
crafts and Birkenstock shoes)
OWNER: Mary Mykytyn
SIZE: Very small
SPECIAL SERVICES: Special orders
SPECIAL EVENTS: N/A
GETTING THERE: Jane subway station, Jane Street
bus; parking on street

Wind in the Willows' display window combines its
three principal businesses: books, beads, and Birkenstock shoes. This is a cheerful store with framed paintings of carousel horses on the wall. The book collection
contains works from Kid's Can Press, Scholastic, Firefly
Press, University of Toronto Press, and Oxford University Press, presented on bookshelves and in several
circular stands.

WONDER WORKS

79A Harbord Street
(near Spadina)
Toronto, Ontario M5S 1G4
416-323-3131 (FAX 416-323-1231)

SPECIALTY: "Inviting a return to the sacred"
OWNER: Mary Anderson
SIZE: Very small
SPECIAL SERVICES: Mail orders, special orders,
bibliographies
SPECIAL EVENTS: N/A
GETTING THERE: Spadina subway station on the
Bloor line; parking on street

An aquarium, the delicate aroma of incense, and soft
background music encourage a state of relaxation
for the patrons of Wonder Works. The store offers a
small collection of books and magazines on alternative
spirituality, including alternative psychology and transpersonal psychology, alternative health and herbal
medicine, women's health issues, women's spirituality,
and spiritual traditions in general. The store carries a
variety of relaxation, lecture, and storytelling tapes as
well as tapes of chanting and folk music. One may also
purchase oils and flower essences for homeopathic
medicine, healing gemstones, incense, small statuaries,
homemade jewellery and dozens of kinds of tarot cards.

More Selection in Every Section

Visit the World's Biggest Bookstore
for the best stories on and off campus.
Over a million books including fiction, art, business and computers,
reference and others.
We have what's on your reading list - and a lot more.

World's Biggest Bookstore

20 Edward Street,
(One block north of the Eaton Centre)
Monday - Saturday : 9:00 a.m. - 10:00 p.m. / Sunday : Noon - 6:00 p.m.
Phone : 977-7009

THE WORLDHOUSE

195 College Street, second floor
(between Beverly and St. George)
Toronto, Ontario M5T 1P9
416-408-4263 (FAX 416-408-4600)
e-mail: games@worldhouse.magic.ca
http://www.worldhouse.magic.ca

SPECIALTY: Dungeons and Dragons, role-playing games, war games, science fiction and fantasy games, trading card games, family games, magazines, miniatures
STAFF: Merle von Thorn, Cheryl Freedman, Alex von Thorn
SIZE: Small
SPECIAL SERVICES: E-mail orders, mail orders
SPECIAL EVENTS: Author signings, card trading days, game demonstrations
GETTING THERE: Queen's Park subway station, College streetcar; parking on side streets

Once there was only Dungeons and Dragons for those wishing to play out fantasy adventures rather than simply read about them. Now there are over one hundred role-playing games in print, the bulk of them produced by a handful of major companies. In general, each game requires a referee and three to six players. Given the episodic nature of the games, they may go on for months, even years, at a time. (The proprietor knows of one game that has been in progress for some twenty years). Most role-playing games are in book form, hence their inclusion in this guide. The Worldhouse is one of the city's leading suppliers of role-playing games. The store also has a web site. In place of the usual bookstore cats, The Worldhouse has a pair of ferrets.

WORLD'S BIGGEST BOOKSTORE

20 Edward Street
(near Yonge, one block north of Dundas)
Toronto, Ontario M5G 1C9
416-977-7009 (FAX 416-977-3728)
BBS 416-581-0052

SPECIALTY: General, with particular strengths in computer books, business, travel, children's books, and around 5,000 magazines
OWNER: Chapters Inc.; Ross Gorrie, manager
SIZE: Very large (over 160,000 titles)
SPECIAL SERVICES: Special orders, mail orders, fax orders, BBS service
SPECIAL EVENTS: Many book signings
GETTING THERE: Dundas subway station; metered parking on street

The World's Biggest Bookstore represents Toronto's first superstore, the very large bookstores that may gradually alter the nature of the bookselling business. One wanders through 65,000 square feet of displays, divided into seventy categories, some as large as a separate specialty bookstore. The World's Biggest Bookstore stocks an enormous number of current titles. In a single stop, one can check the most recent publications in categories ranging from art, business, and childcare to sports, travel, and war. The store also maintains a large backlist and sells great quantities of sale and promotional books. Other products sold include magazines, books on tape, maps, videos, and computer software.

WRITERS AND COMPANY: THE LITERARY BOOKSTORE

2005 Yonge Street
(two blocks west of Davisville)
Toronto, Ontario M4S 1Z8
416-481-8432 (No FAX)

SPECIALTY: Fiction, poetry, literary theory, baseball, jazz, children's literature, travel narratives
OWNERS: Winston Smith and Susan Folkins
SIZE: Medium (around 30,000 titles)
SPECIAL SERVICES: Special orders, mail orders, school and library consulting, book group consulting
SPECIAL EVENTS: Book launches
GETTING THERE: Davisville subway station; metered parking on street

Writers and Company looks like the kind of private library any bibliophile would love to own, given sufficient space: serious, restful, attractive. Wooden bookcases rise seven shelves high, with single titles displayed spine out. There are four bookcases devoted to poetry, two to criticism, seventeen to fiction, five to new fiction, one to baseball (both literature and trivia), and one to jazz. Small, waist-high bookcases display anthologies, children's books, and travel books. In the front of the store, one finds books on writing, women's studies, and social commentary. There are so many titles you'd like to peruse that leaving the store becomes very difficult. You might as well pick out a few volumes, sit down on the park bench thoughtfully provided (near a framed hanging sign reading, "So many books, so little time"), and make your selection carefully.

YESTERDAY'S HEROES

742 Bathurst Street
(near Bloor)
Toronto, Ontario M5S 2R5
416-533-9800 (FAX 416-533-1737)

SPECIALTY: Buy and sell new and used comics, sports cards, role-playing games, toys
OWNER: George Amaral
SIZE: Large
SPECIAL SERVICES: Memberships, discounts, reserving service
SPECIAL EVENTS: Monthly sales on the first weekend of the month
GETTING THERE: One block south of Bathurst subway station; parking in lots

Yesterday's Heroes occupies a long, narrow store with posters on display and many, many bins of comics. Under "S" I noted a number of titles not frequently encountered elsewhere: *Sabre, Samurai, Savage Dragon, Scout, Secret Origins, Sgt. Fury, Sgt. Rock, Shatter, Sherlock Holmes, Sleep Walker, Speed Racer, Spell Jammer, Spirits Vengeance, Star Slayer, Storm Watch, Suicide Squad, Super Soldier,* and *Super Patriot.* In addition to an impressive number of Silver Age (ca. 1956–1970) and Golden Age (ca. 1945–1956) back issues, the store carries trade paperbacks, graphic novels, Archie books, Dr. Who books, Star Wars and Star Trek magazines and other paraphernalia, sports and non-sport cards, and action figures.

YORK UNIVERSITY BOOKSTORE

4700 Keele Street (at Steeles)
Toronto, Ontario M3J 1P3
416-736-5024 (FAX 416-736-5733)
e-mail: bookstor@yorku.ca
http://booknode.extrel.yorku.ca/

SPECIALTY: General academic bookstore, with an emphasis on scholarly books
OWNER: York University
SIZE: Large
SPECIAL SERVICES: Special orders
SPECIAL EVENTS: Book launches
GETTING THERE: Downsview subway station, then #106 bus; short-term parking north of bookstore

The newly revitalized York University Bookstore displays its books on tables, in pyramids, in circular stands, in standing boxes, and in stylized "popcorn stands" in addition to the traditional labelled bookcases. The collection includes more than fifty categories of books and is especially strong in the social sciences. Many selections could be found in any large general bookstore, but the emphasis of the collection on academic books marks this as a first-rate university bookstore. Textbooks are located on the lower level, and there is the usual section of stationery, student supplies, etc. A branch of the bookstore may be found at the Glendon College campus at 2275 Bayview Avenue, at Lawrence (416-487-6702).

MAIL-ORDER
BOOKSTORES

AFTERWORDS

Box 657, Station P
Toronto, Ontario M5S 2Y4
416-588-6663 (No FAX)
e-mail: dalopes@io.org

SPECIALTY: New and used small and underground press literature, with a focus on Canadian authors
OWNER: Damian Lopes
SIZE: Small (around 1,000 items)
SPECIAL SERVICES: Mail orders, want lists
SPECIAL EVENTS: N/A

The 1960s in Canada saw the birth of a number of small and underground presses such as bpNichol's Ganglia Press, and, later, John Curry's Curved Hands Press. The output of these presses, frequently as few as a hundred copies of a book, are not generally available in bookstores. Damian Lopes began by collecting these works and, more recently, has become a distributor through his bookstore. Where Lopes might once have bought a single copy from a small press, now he purchases two or three, lists them in his catalogues, and sells them to others interested in this specialized field. In so doing, he performs a genuine service to the small presses, many of which have no formal distribution system for their product. Those interested in learning more about Lopes' stock can request a catalogue by mail, telephone, or e-mail.

ALMARK & COMPANY, BOOKSELLERS

P.O. Box 7
Thornhill, Ontario L3T 3N1
905-764-2665 (FAX 905-764-5571)
e-mail: 75711.2144@compuserve.com

SPECIALTY: Modern first editions, all genres
OWNER: Al Navis
SIZE: Large
SPECIAL SERVICES: Search service in specialties
VISITORS: By appointment only

Al Navis has perfected the art of mail-order service for the book collector. In place of catalogues, he issues stock lists giving a description of each copy of each book he holds by the requested author, with more than 750 authors in the areas of general fiction and literature, science fiction and fantasy, historical fiction, mystery, crime and detective fiction, dark fantasy and horror fiction, and military fiction. Navis also issues selected sub-genre stock lists in Black fiction and literature, Canadian fiction and literature, Kennedy assassinations, Winston Churchill, and several other topics. Collectors interested in works of Iris Murdoch or Len Deighton or Salman Rushdie, for example, can receive instant answers to specific questions, since all the information is on-line, or a stock list by mail or facsimile. The stock list for John Updike, for example, lists three copies of *Rabbit Redux*: a second impression of the first edition, a third impression of the first edition, and the first British edition. In addition to his bookselling business, Al Navis does a weekly radio program on sports books, *Between the Lines*, for the FAN–590.

ALPHABET BOOKSHOP

145 Main Street West
Port Colborne, Ontario L3K 3V3
905-834-5323 (FAX same)
e-mail: alphabet@iaw.on.ca

CCH CANADIAN LIMITED

SPECIALTY: Modern first editions, letters, rare books, illustrated books, jazz and beat
OWNER: Richard Shuh and Linda Woolley
SIZE: Medium
SPECIAL SERVICES: N/A
SPECIAL EVENTS: N/A

The Alphabet Bookshop retains its sign from the days when it operated on Harbord Street in Toronto, but the sign is now displayed only inside the store, which operates primarily as a mail-order business out of a private home. The owners handle twentieth-century first editions, many of them signed by the author, in the areas of poetry, fiction, jazz, American, Canadian, and British literature, Black literature, and South American literature, and produce catalogues in these areas six times a year.

For CCH Canadian Limited, see preceding section on Retail Bookstores (page 53).

C.W. HAY BOOKSELLER

Midtown Mall, 200 John Street West
Oshawa, Ontario L1J 2B4
1-800-567-0568 (FAX 905-728-6351)
e-mail: webmaster@mail.cwhay.com
http://www.cwhay.com

SPECIALTY: Mail order for any book in print in
North America
OWNER: Bill Hay
SIZE: Medium (30,000 titles in stock)
SPECIAL SERVICES: E-mail and mail orders,
specializing in hard-to-get items

Of the 250 bookstores included in this book, C.W. Hay Bookseller is the only one we visited only in its electronic incarnation. The store's home page, in its current form, offers a description of the store and its services, and a form for ordering books. Future plans for the web site include electronic browsing capability. If you don't have Internet access, the store will respond to your requests by mail, telephone, or fax (or you can visit the store in person). The store will obtain the volume and send it to you using the CANPAR courier service, and charge your VISA, MasterCard, or American Express credit card.

CEC PUBLISHING

8101, boulevard Métropolitain Est
Anjou, Québec H1J 1J9
416-323-1822 or 1-800-268-9715
(FAX 514-351-3534)

SPECIALTY: French educational books
OWNER: CEC Inc.
SIZE: Medium

For teachers of French in English-speaking Canadian public schools, French-immersion programs, or schools in the province of Québec, CEC (Centre Éducatif et Culturel) offers a variety of learning materials. Its catalogue is divided into preschool, French, French for immersion classes, French as a second language, English as a second language, science, mathematics, religious instruction, social sciences, and studio art. These materials include texts and workbooks, dictionaries, grammar books, reading and writing guides, and teachers' manuals, each aimed at a particular grade level. Other catalogues are available for French at the university level. All the materials sold have been approved by the Québec Ministry of Education and many ministries of educations in other provinces. CEC Publishing is also the distributor for Hachette (France) for its pedagogical materials.

CANADIAN PROFESSIONAL INFORMATION CENTRE LTD.

For Canadian Professional Information Centre Ltd., see preceding section on Retail Bookstores (page 55).

THE CAN-DO BOOKSTORE

276 Delaware Avenue
Toronto, Ontario M6H 2T6
416-538-3157 (No FAX)

SPECIALTY: Woodworking, fabric, and crafts
OWNER: Stan Adelman
SIZE: Small (3,000 titles)
SPECIAL SERVICES: Mail orders, delivery, 10% discount to libraries, schools, and institutions
SPECIAL EVENTS: N/A

The Can-Do Bookstore sells "books for people who like to do things," particularly those interested in woodworking. Owner Stan Adelman issues a short, descriptive catalogue of books in general woodworking techniques, tools, woodturning, scrollsaw patterns, small projects, carving, bird carving, wood identification, home construction, and musical instrument construction. He also offers to prepare a list of books tailored to individual needs. Adelman serves as the area distributor for the Sterling Craftsman Book Catalogue, which offers hundreds of titles in woodworking, cabinetmaking, furniture, woodfinishing, and related subjects.

CHILD'S PLAY

120 Watline Avenue
Mississauga, Ontario L4Z 2C1
905-890-8111 (FAX 905-890-3149)

SPECIALTY: Books, games, and audiovisual materials
OWNER: Child's Play (International) Ltd.
SIZE: Medium
SPECIAL SERVICES: Mail orders

Child's Play is a mail-order firm specializing in materials for younger children, including baby carriage books (equipped with fastenings to prevent their being thrown overboard), bath books (printed on padded vinyl), board books, activity books, early reading (connecting pictures with words), die-cut books (to develop familiarity with names and shapes of letters or words), play books, information books, and the Child's Play Library of storybooks. The firm also sells video and audio cassettes, games, musical instruments, French editions, and books on life skills and responsibility, designed to combat prejudice and develop positive attitudes.

CHRIST THE WAY PUBLICATIONS

Box 43120, Eastwood Square
Kitchener, Ontario N2H 6S9
519-576-2600 (FAX 519-576-3808)

SPECIALTY: Gospel tracts
OWNER: Limited corporation
SIZE: Small

Christ the Way Publications serves as the Canadian distributor for Chick Publications of Chino, California, an extreme right-wing publisher of Gospel tracts in cartoon form. The catalogue offers hints for spreading the gospel by leaving Chick tracts in public places. The literature fervently opposes Roman Catholicism and all other "false religions" (Mormons, Jehovah's Witnesses, Hindus, New Agers, Buddhists, and Muslims), as well as the ecumenical movement, rock music, cults and the occult, the theory of evolution, and much more. Tracts are available in English and in forty-four other languages.

THE COMFORTABLE CHOICE

1001 Bay Street, Suite 410
Toronto, Ontario M5S 3A6
416-928-5924 (FAX 416-928-9354)

SPECIALTY: Large-print books
OWNER: P.C. Leong
SIZE: Small
SPECIAL SERVICES: mail-order only, money-back
   guarantee

The Comfortable Choice sells large-print books on a variety of subjects, including the latest best-sellers. The books are not limited to the visually challenged, but are for anybody who finds it more comfortable to read large print. The catalogue includes titles of books in biography and autobiography, Canadian classics, cooking, gardening, health and fitness, humour, inspirational works, romantic novels, travel, and current best-sellers.

COMPUBOOKSTORE

c/o CompuFamily, Inc.
235 Yorkland Boulevard, Suite 300
North York, Ontario M2J 4Y8
416-493-5193 (FAX 416-491-2757)
e-mail: order@compubookstore.com

SPECIALTY: Computer books
OWNER: David Chen
SIZE: N/A
SPECIAL SERVICES: E-mail orders

Primarily a digital bookstore, CompuBookStore began selling only computer books via an electronic bulletin board. It has now expanded its scope of operations to include English-language books in print available in North America, and has enlarged its access to include regular mail, telephone, and fax as well as e-mail. The store maintains an informal dialogue with its customers, via whichever channel they choose to communicate, and promises speedy delivery of books.

FRIENDS OF TERPSICHORE

836–20 Carlton Street
Toronto, Ontario M5B 2H5
416-348-0896 (FAX 416-340-9958)

SPECIALTY: Secondhand and out-of-print books on dance
OWNER: Maria Los and Carol Los
SIZE: Small
SPECIAL SERVICES: N/A

Originally a bookstore on Yonge Street, Friends of Terpsichore now operates as a mail-order firm serving Canadian and American universities, Canadian dance schools, and film-makers. Their book list includes dance biographies and autobiographies about Isadora Duncan, Tamara Karsavina, and Fred Astaire; books on dance training, including tap dancing, ice dancing, ballet, roller disco dancing, and techniques of dance notation; dance history and aesthetics, from *Balanchine's New Complete Stories of the Great Ballets* to *Folk Dances of the British Isles* and *Clog Dances in the Appalachians*. The owners also accept visitors by appointment.

GIROL BOOKS, INC.

P.O. Box 5473, Station F
Ottawa, Ontario K2C 3M1
613-233-9044 (FAX same)

SPECIALTY: Spanish-language books, magazines, and newspapers and Portuguese-language books
OWNER: Leslie Roster, manager
SIZE: Medium
SPECIAL SERVICES: Mail orders
SPECIAL EVENTS: N/A

Girol Books imports and distributes books in Spanish from Spain and Latin America. The collection ranges from the classics to contemporary works by Isabel Allende, Laura Esquivel, Mario Vargas Llosa, Gabriel García Márquez, Eduardo Mendoza, Rosa Montero, et al. Girol also carries Spanish translations of English-language mysteries, science fiction novels, romances, adventures, and spy novels. In addition to fiction, the store carries books in poetry, theatre, and essays. Among general interest categories, Girol sells Spanish-language books on biography, child care, cooking, games, health, popular psychology, and self-improvement. For those studying the Spanish language, Girol can supply dictionaries, grammars, exercise books, textbooks, self-study courses with cassettes, and easy-reading or adapted books for beginning readers. For professionals working in translation, Girol carries specialized bilingual or multilingual dictionaries covering such fields as law, computer technology, business, finance, and international relations. Girol publishes Latin American theatre, theatre criticism, and multi-cultural books, and represents Canadian Spanish-language small presses. In addition, Girol carries a substantial selection of books in Portuguese from Portugal and Brazil.

GULLIVER'S TRAVEL BOOK SHOP

416-537-7700 (No FAX)

SPECIALTY: Travel books, history, geography, flags and emblems
OWNER: Louise Field
SIZE: "Lilliputian"
SPECIAL SERVICES: Mail orders, searches, special orders

Collecting flags used to be the hobby of the proprietor of Gulliver's Travel Book Shop. Now it has become a distinguishing feature of the store, which can supply flags in all sizes for cities, provinces, and countries. You can plan a trip with travel guides, picture books, videos and maps for walking tours, drives on country roads, historical tours, theme tours, sightseeing trips, or travels off the beaten track. Having equipped yourself with the necessary travel accessories (money belts, electricity converters, dictionaries, and phrase books), you can fill the time left before your trip reading tales of travel in the region of your destination. While it seeks a new retail location, the book shop takes orders by telephone and delivers by mail or courier.

HAMPSTEAD HOUSE BOOKS, LTD.

82 Doncaster Avenue
Thornhill, Ontario L3T 7S3
895-771-0607 (FAX 905-881-6596)

SPECIALTY: Remainder books
OWNER: Private corporation
SIZE: Medium
SPECIAL SERVICES: Money-back guarantee

Hampstead House specializes in publishers' remainders, also known as publishers' inventory clearances, warehouse clearances, and publishers' overstock. These are new books which, for one reason or another, did not sell well through local bookstores and were returned to the publisher. Tax laws on warehouse stock make it advantageous for publishers to offer these books at substantial discounts, either through bookstores or through mail-order firms such as Hampstead House. Interested readers can find titles ranging from *Life in the Castle in Medieval England* to *Death by Chocolate*, a recipe book, to *E.M. Forster: Three Complete Novels*, all at greatly reduced prices.

JOHN RUSH

116 Eastbourne Avenue
Hamilton, Ontario L8M 2M8
905-545-0661 (No fax)

SPECIALTY: Canadiana and general antiquarian
books
OWNER: John Rush
SIZE: Small (around 1,500 titles)
SPECIAL SERVICES: Mail orders
SPECIAL EVENTS: N/A
GETTING THERE: Visit by appointment only

Contrary to expectations, rare books are not necessarily expensive. John Rush seeks out curiosities of Canadiana, such as *My First Christmas Memory during the Chicago Fire of 1871* by Martha Louise Black, the first MP from the Yukon, or *The Story of Mimico — Home of the Wild Pigeon* by Edwin Eland. Monthly catalogues list selections from Rush's current stock, with an average price of around $70, which he sells to institutional collectors and libraries, private collectors, and historians interested in details of local history. Rush does a brisk trade in appalling poetry and notes that while crummy poetry is in great demand, the good stuff is never read. (He has presentation copies of books from one poet to another that have obviously never been opened.) Rush's catalogues, which include numbers of books published by Canadian small presses, or self-published by authors, make fascinating reading in their own right.

JOSEPH PATRICK BOOKS

P.O. Box 100, Station V
Toronto, Ontario M6R 3A4
416-766-3357 (No fax)

SPECIALTY: Canadiana, local histories, autographs,
exploration and travel, Catholica
OWNER: J.G. Sherlock
SIZE: Medium
SPECIAL SERVICES: Mail orders, searches, appraisals
SPECIAL EVENTS: N/A
GETTING THERE: By appointment only

Making a living selling Canadiana has become more difficult as the proportion of the population with its roots in Canada has declined. With Steven Temple and Nelson Ball specializing in Canadian literature, Joseph Patrick Books has found its niche in other aspects of Canadiana. Its holdings include a substantial amount of Arctic material, some of it resulting from the sale of the Hudson's Bay Library, as well as rare pamphlets, broadsides, ephemera, and early Canadian printed material. Its stock comes from private collectors, other dealers, book fairs, and nostalgia shows. The store sells mostly to institutional collectors such as universities and government archives. Call proprietor J.G. Sherlock for a catalogue or to arrange and appointment.

LETTERS BOOKSELLER

77 Florence Street, Studio 104
Toronto, Ontario M6K 1P4
416-537-5403 (No FAX)

SPECIALTY: Rare literature, modern poetry, the small press, printed literary ephemera, collections
OWNER: Nick Drumbolis
SIZE: Medium (35,000 volumes)
SPECIAL SERVICES: Compiles and produces book lists of Canadian small presses, past and present, and histories of the alternative literary scene in Canada; curates the Small Press Resource Centre
SPECIAL EVENTS: Toronto Small Press Group semi-annual bookfairs

Nick Drumbolis distinguishes between what he calls distributive bookstores, meaning stores that sell any book they can, and contributive bookstores, such as his own, which focus on "culturally resonant stocks." Since 1982, Letters has served as a depot for esoteric literature, and a forum for cultural discourse and events. The latter function has declined as the store has diminished its walk-in business, but it remains a flourishing concern as repository for small press and esoteric books (those produced less for commercial than aesthetic reasons), issuing regular catalogues of selections of stock for sale. By appointment only.

MOBILE BOOK STORE

524 Concession Street
Hamilton, Ontario L8V 1A6
905-318-6811 or 1-800-387-7916
(FAX 905-318-6883)

SPECIALTY: Bahá'i literature and audiovisual materials
OWNER: Barney and Nancy Barnhart
SIZE: Small
SPECIAL SERVICES: Mail orders
SPECIAL EVENTS: N/A

The Mobile Bookstore, open for retail business five days a week in Hamilton, operates a mail-order business of interest to Toronto customers. The store specializes in the distribution of Bahá'i literature including sacred writings (original writings of the Báb, Bah'u'lláh and combinations of their writings in prayerbooks, etc.), writings of Shoghi Effendi, writings of the Universal House of Justice, compilations from the writings, histories of the major figures of the faith and of the faith itself, children's books, specialties (puzzles, calendars, stickers, computer programs), and audiovisual materials including cassettes and compact discs. The store issues regular catalogues containing both booklists and detailed descriptions of selected items.

Nelson Ball, Bookseller

USED AND RARE BOOKS

31 Willow Street, Paris, Ontario N3L 2K7
Telephone: (519) 442-6113

CANADIAN LITERATURE

POETRY
DRAMA
FICTION
FICTION SET IN CANADA
ESSAYS
QUEBEC AUTHORS IN ENGLISH TRANSLATION
LITERARY ANTHOLOGIES
LITERARY HISTORY AND CRITICISM
LITERARY BIOGRAPHY AND BIBLIOGRAPHY
LITERARY PERIODICALS

Special sections include:

GRAPHIC PUBLISHERS
COACH HOUSE PRESS
JUVENILE FICTION
STEPHEN LEACOCK
BPNICHOL
PAPERBACK FICTION
PROOFS AND ADVANCE COPIES

Customers welcome to visit by appointment
Mail order
Catalogues issued
Appraisal of literary papers

NELSON BALL, BOOKSELLER

31 Willow Street
Paris, Ontario N3L 2K7
519-442-6113 (No FAX)

SPECIALTY: Canadian literature (used and rare)
OWNER: Nelson Ball
SIZE: Medium
SPECIAL SERVICES: Mail orders
SPECIAL EVENTS: N/A
GETTING THERE: Visit by appointment only

Nelson Ball carries one of the largest stocks of Canadian literature in the country, with a specialty in modern Canadian poetry (1930 to the present). His holdings in poetry alone number some 3,500 titles of books and pamphlets, or 4,000 including broadsides and leaflets. From 1972 to 1984, Ball operated his business in Toronto under the name William Nelson Books. Rarities he has bought and sold include the first issue of Crawford's *Old Spookses' Pass* and two copies of Pratt's *Rachel*. Ball carries an unusually large selection of books and pamphlets by bpNichol. In 1985, he moved to Paris, where he carries on the business from his home. Ball sells to readers, writers, collectors, academics, and to public and university libraries, and regularly issues catalogues of poetry and fiction.

PETER L. JACKSON MILITARY BOOKS

23 Castle Green Crescent
Toronto, Ontario M9R 1N5
416-249-4796 (No FAX)

SPECIALTY: Rare and out-of-print military and naval books bought and sold
OWNER: Peter L. Jackson
SIZE: Small (3,000 to 4,000 titles in stock)
SPECIAL SERVICES: Issues two catalogues a year; visitors by appointment

Peter L. Jackson's most recent catalogue, the forty-eighth issued, lists more than 1,400 military books along with information primarily intended for collectors (date of publication, a brief description of the contents, format, condition, price), with entries subdivided into military history to 1914, Napoleonic wars, Famous Regiments series, World War I, World War II, post-war campaigns and addenda, and books by A.A. Osprey. Jackson maintains a large stock of books in his specialty and welcomes visitors by appointment, although the major part of his business is by mail order.

ST. NICHOLAS BOOKS

P.O. Box 863, Station F

Toronto, Ontario M4Y 2N7

416-922-6940 (No FAX)

SPECIALTY: Children's books and related ephemera and bibliography

OWNER: Yvonne Knight

SIZE: Small

SPECIAL SERVICES: Operates by mail and by appointment

St. Nicholas Books specializes in 20th-century children's books. In contrast to the other children's bookstores described in this guide, St. Nicholas Books deals primarily with collectors seeking first editions of out-of-print books. Owner Yvonne Knight issues regular catalogues (the most recent are numbered 49 and 50) with detailed descriptions of the books, their size, format, and condition. The store operates primarily as a mail-order business with an international clientele, but the owner will receive visitors by appointment.

TERRIFIC TITLES FOR YOUNG READERS

52 Hazelton Avenue

Toronto, Ontario M5R 2E2

416-921-9557 (FAX 416-921-0408)

SPECIALTY: Children's books

OWNER: Privately owned

SIZE: Small

SPECIAL SERVICES: Cataloguing available for all titles

Terrific Titles for Young Readers supplies children's books for libraries and individual readers. The current catalogue offers detailed descriptions and cover illustrations for Canadian reference books, picture books, activity books, and books on fiction, history, legends, native people, natural history, poetry, science, and sports, as well as a checklist of some 600 titles. Individual entries give recommended ages, date of publication (but not the publisher), number of pages, and price.

ULVERSCROFT LARGE PRINT BOOKS, LTD.

P.O. Box 80038
Burlington, Ontario L7L 6B1
905-637-8734 (FAX 905-333-6788)

SPECIALTY: Large-print books
OWNER: The Ulverscroft Foundation
SIZE: Small
SPECIAL SERVICES: Standing order discounts

Ulverscroft is a non-profit foundation established in the United Kingdom to provide material for the visually challenged. It offers large-print books in several lines: Charnwood, for contemporary fiction; non-fiction; Ulverscroft, described as "a good read"; the Linford (softcover) series of romances, mysteries, and westerns; a new Niagara series, featuring American and Canadian authors; and a line of Canadian books in French. Ulverscroft also carries Soundings audiobooks of unabridged, single-voice readings and Magna Story Sound spoken-word cassettes. Quarterly catalogues offer extended descriptions of available titles, issued at the rate of 444 titles per year. A stock list contains a cumulative catalogue of some 3,000 available books.

WHOLE CHILD

P.O. Box 100
Campbellville, Ontario LOP 1B0
1-800-387-2888 (FAX 905-854-2090)

SPECIALTY: Books for gentle parenting, activities for creative play
OWNER: Dean Boyd
SIZE: Small
SPECIAL SERVICES: Mail-order catalogue

Whole Child has as its mission to provide carefully selected material and products that support children's self-esteem and well-being and encourage positive family interaction. The "Parenting" section of the catalogue offers books for celebrating our children, creative learning, gentle birth and bonding, expressing feelings and learning social skills, healthy family relationships, health and safety, parent well-being, parenting older children, play therapy, peacemaking skills, raising responsible, ethical and self-reliant children, self-help for kids and teens, and special needs and circumstances. In addition, *Whole Child* offers scaled down "real" carpentry tools, looms and other handcrafts, a large selection of wooden toys, unconventional children's books, and books of family activities.

OUT-OF-TOWN BOOKSTORES

Selected bookstores within a short
drive of the city of Toronto

CHAPTERS

Woodview Place, 3315 Fairview Street
(at Cumberland)
Burlington, Ontario L7N 3N9
905-681-2410 (FAX 905-681-8618)

SPECIALTY: General bookstore
OWNER: Chapters (Head Office, 90 Ronson Drive,
Rexdale, Ontario M9W ICI, telephone
416-243-3138, FAX 416-243-8964)
SIZE: Very large (over 100,000 titles)
SPECIAL SERVICES: Special order anything in print
SPECIAL EVENTS: Storytelling for children,
activities and crafts, author readings, information
sessions and workshop, band concerts
GETTING THERE: Parking in mall

Chapters, the chain of book superstores, is in the
process of establishing units all across Canada, with
Toronto stores due to open at 110 Bloor Street and at
Yonge and Steeles at about the time this guide appears.
The Burlington store occupies an area that one would
ordinarily associate more with a department store than
with a bookstore, but after the shock of the sheer size
wears off, one notices comfortable reading chairs
throughout and direct access to Starbucks Coffee when
you get tired of walking. The major sections consist of
multimedia, fiction and literature, best-sellers (25%
off), reading and writing, lifestyle, My Books (an enormous children's section), and Newsstand (with more
than 1,400 magazines). The directory at the front of the
store explains the division of 100,000 books into 250
categories. The walls of the store are covered with
literary riddles (e.g., "In Stendhal's *The Charterhouse of
Parma*, what is a charterhouse?" Answer: a monastery).
Keep an eye on the time when you visit Chapters; you
may find yourself spending the entire day here.

A DIFFERENT DRUMMER

513 Locust Street
Burlington, Ontario L7S 1V3
905-639-0925 (FAX 905-681-8893)

SPECIALTY: "Good books on all subjects"
OWNER: Richard Bachmann
SIZE: Medium
SPECIAL SERVICES: Special orders, corporate
accounts, mail orders, newsletter
SPECIAL EVENTS: Longest-running author reading
series in Canada
GETTING THERE: Municipal parking lot beside store

The store's name comes from Thoreau's *Walden*: "If a
man does not keep pace with his companions, perhaps
it is because he hears a different drummer." There is
something unmistakably fresh and new about this
store, partly because of the posters, the unusual design,
the discreet lighting and background sounds of cham-
ber music or jazz, but primarily in the attractive covers
of good books displayed face out. Twenty-five years ago
an architect transformed a brick house into this bookstore which, like the Guggenheim Museum, can be best
appreciated by starting at the top and working your
way down the spiral. At the upper level, near comfortable reading chairs often inhabited by the bookstore
cats, I saw shelved sections on literary criticism and
philosophy. Books displayed on the staircase wall come
into view as one descends to a large section of children's
books on the middle floor. On the main level of the
store one finds books on a variety of topics, all reflecting
a very discriminating taste. At A Different Drummer
one doesn't need to wade through the dross, but can
simply revel in the pleasure of seeing a myriad of good
books. *The Drummer Gazette*, describing the reading
series and certain new books, appears three times a year.

JOAN DRAPER, BOOKSELLER

267 Victoria Street, P.O. Box 729
Niagara-on-the-Lake, Ontario L0S 1J0
905-468-7885 (FAX 905-468-3777)

SPECIALTY: General used books (special interest in Bloomsbury)
OWNER: Joan Draper, ABAC
SIZE: Small
SPECIAL SERVICES: Special order
SPECIAL EVENTS: N/A

Niagara-on-the-Lake, one of Ontario's most charming towns, offers country inns, restaurants, wineries, and the theatres of the Shaw Festival in addition to its interesting shops and bookstores. Joan Draper displays a small, well-chosen collection of hardcover books, many in their original dustjackets, in a number of areas: arts and crafts, biography, Canadian and American history, essays and poetry, fiction, history (especially British), music and art, nature, navigation and yachting, religion and travel. Many of the books are quite recent, including a 1992 biography of Benjamin Britten. There are a few rare books, notably *Tales of the Genii*, published in 1764. Any booklover could find something of interest here.

OLD NIAGARA BOOKSHOP

44 Queen Street
Niagara-on-the-Lake, Ontario L0S 1J0
905-468-2602 (No FAX)

SPECIALTY: General books, hardcover and paperback, with a predominance of trade paperback books
OWNER: Laura MacFadden
SIZE: Small
SPECIAL SERVICES: Special orders
SPECIAL EVENTS: N/A

In an age of computerized inventory and transactions, Laura MacFadden operates her bookstore the old way, writing receipts by hand at an antique desk. The books are organized into general areas, but without labels, in order to encourage browsing and leave the owner free to arrange books in a variety of ways. The store carries a general stock, with particular strengths in art, biography, Canadian literature, travel, and works by and about George Bernard Shaw, subject of the local Shaw Festival. A separate room contains a large selection of children's books, its bookcases bedecked with stuffed dolls ranging from an Alice based on Tenniel (not Disney) to Waldo of "Where's Waldo"?

WILLIAM MATTHEWS, BOOKSELLER

16 Jarvis Street
Fort Erie, Ontario L2A 2S1
905-871-8484 (FAX 905-871-9857)

SPECIALTY: General used and rare books; sensational fiction and early fantasy
OWNER: William Matthews and Ann Hall
SIZE: Large (around 100,000 books)
SPECIAL SERVICES: N/A
SPECIAL EVENTS: N/A

William Matthews operates two rather different businesses. The bookstore, formerly at Queen and Parliament Streets in Toronto, now located in a row of thrift stores in Fort Erie, contains an enormous stock of general used books of varying quality purchased from estates or passing customers. A member of the Antiquarian Booksellers' Association of Canada, Matthews sells used and rare books with a specialty in fantasy and science fiction books and pulp magazines for collectors, a field represented in Toronto by Jamie Fraser. Matthews issues catalogues detailing the publication information, format, condition and price of these books, many of them quite rare.

GEOGRAPHICAL INDEX

Geographical Index

This geographical index divides the city into eleven sections, some consisting of a narrow corridor, others including a wider region. Within each area, bookstores are listed under the categories General, Used & Rare, Specialty, and Comics. (This geographical index includes only bookstores in the greater Toronto area. For mail-order bookstores, see page 141. For out-of-town bookstores, see page 157.)

Metro Centre

Bounded by Yonge Street to the east, University Avenue/Avenue Road to the west, St. Clair to the north, the Lake to the south

GENERAL

USED & RARE

SPECIALTY

COMICS

Metro East

Bounded by the Lake to the east, Yonge Street to the west,
Bloor Street/Danforth to the north, the Lake to the south

Metro West

Bounded by University Avenue to the east, the Kingsway to the west, Bloor Street to the north, and the Lake to the south

Bloor East

*Bloor Street/Danforth Avenue bounded by Kingston Road
to the east and Yonge Street to the west*

Bloor West

*Bloor Street bounded by Yonge Street to the east
and the Kingsway to the west*

Queen East

Queen Street East bounded by Yonge Street to the west and Victoria Park Avenue to the east

GENERAL

The Booksmith 53

USED & RARE

Acadia Book Store 30
Alexandre Fine Antique Maps and Books 33
Bookland 50
Kew Beach Galleries 82

SPECIALTY

Champlain Book Store/Librairie Champlain 56
The Toy Circus 123

Queen West

Queen Street West bounded by University Avenue to the east and Lake Shore Boulevard to the west

GENERAL

Pages Books and Magazines 99

USED & RARE

Abelard Books 29
David Mason Books 67
Jamie Fraser Books 81
McBurnie and Cutler 90
Robert Wright Books 107
Steven Temple Books 115
Village Book Store 131

SPECIALTY

Arka Ukrainian Books 38
Art Metropole 39
Bakka Science Fiction Book Shoppe 43
Chan Sheung Kee Book Co. 57
Garden Room Books 74

COMICS

Alternate Gravity 34
Dragon Lady Comic Shop 69
Grey Region 76
Silver Snail 111

North

Bounded by Yonge Street to the east, Avenue Road to the west, Steeles Avenue to the north, and St. Clair Avenue to the south

North East

Bounded by Markham Road to the east, Yonge Street to the west, Steeles Avenue to the north and Bloor Street/Danforth Avenue to the south

North West

Bounded by Avenue Road to the east, Highway 427 to the west, Steeles Avenue to the north and Bloor Street to the south

West

Bounded by the Kingsway to the east, Highway 427 to the west, Bloor Street to the north and the Lake to the south

Markham

GENERAL

Green Gables Books   76

USED & RARE

Alfsen House Books   33

SPECIALTY

The Law Bookstore   85
New Age Books for Transformational Living   94

COMICS

Comic Prince Bookstore   63

Mississauga

SPECIALTY

Canadian Professional Information Centre Ltd.   55

COMICS

Altered States Comics   34

Stouffville-Whitchurch

USED & RARE

John Lord's Books   81

Unionville

SPECIALTY

Annable Nursery Limited   35

SUBJECT GUIDE
TO BOOKSTORES

Subject Guide to Bookstores